The Superparliaments

PRAEGER SPECIAL STUDIES IN
INTERNATIONAL POLITICS AND PUBLIC AFFAIRS

The Superparliaments

INTERPARLIAMENTARY CONSULTATION AND ATLANTIC COOPERATION

J. Allan Hovey, Jr.

FREDERICK A. PRAEGER, Publishers
New York • Washington • London

The purpose of the Praeger Special Studies is to make specialized research monographs in U.S. and international economics and politics available to the academic, business, and government communities. For further information, write to the Special Projects Division, Frederick A. Praeger, Publishers, 111 Fourth Avenue, New York, N.Y. 10003.

FREDERICK A. PRAEGER, PUBLISHERS
111 Fourth Avenue, New York, N.Y. 10003, U.S.A.
77-79 Charlotte Street, London W.1, England

Published in the United States of America in 1966
by Frederick A. Praeger, Inc., Publishers

Second printing, 1967

Library of Congress Catalog Card Number: 66-14088

Printed in the United States of America

To My Parents

PREFACE

What I here call the superparliaments are international regional assemblies of members of national legislatures convened regularly to investigate and debate international problems and to vote resolutions of opinion and recommendation.

There are now six superparliaments in the Atlantic area. At their best they exercise a demonstrable and generally salutary influence on the formulation and the popularization of regional programs and policies. They provide a needed increment of parliamentary oversight and support for a variety of intergovernmental agencies. They are, to be sure, "talking shops," innocent of legislative power, but the modern national parliament began with comparable disabilities, and many hard-headed politicians who serve in today's consultative assemblies are on record as favoring and expecting a comparable evolutionary development.

It is of course important to keep that prospect in perspective. The persistent notion that better political machinery alone can dispose of problems that are rooted in conflicts of interest or doctrine begs a basic question and has led to some rude historical awakenings. It obscures the hard necessity of dealing step by step with issues and, ironically, it does some disservice to the cause of institutional reform itself.

The limits of institutional reform are defined by the underlying consensus about objectives. But within those limits institutions can and must, as Alain Poher has written, be prepared to renew and modernize themselves at a rhythm that is not too far out of phase with that of modern technical achievements.

The past twenty years have witnessed an unparalleled acceleration of international regional cooperation and integration. Intergovernmental agencies have proliferated. In the process, public and parliamentary control has tended to become attenuated. Whether the attenuation is good or bad is no doubt, up to a point, arguable, but beyond that point there stands the unassailable democratic proposition that for an administrative service, as Paul-Henri Spaak has put it, "Fear of a parliament is the beginning of wisdom."

The establishment of the European Community and the emergence of Atlantic "partnership" as a widely accepted Western goal have posed the problem of rationalizing and revitalizing interparliamentary consultation, particularly that involving Western Europe and North America jointly. Despite some notable achievements, the NATO Parliamentarians' Conference has proved relatively unsuccessful in stimulating official action or even response. Spaak, while Secretary General of NATO, had advised Atlantic parliamentarians in 1959 to study the problem in depth and to present "concrete proposals that the governments will be obliged to examine."

Both the European Community and the Atlantic Alliance have recently experienced crises — of a similar nature and a common origin — that suggest basic internal disagreements about objectives and that may therefore rule out, for the present, any prospect of major institutional reform. But as Poher wrote recently with respect to the European Community, of whose Parliament he is President, now is a good time to proceed deliberately and serenely with the study and preparation of next steps.

The legislators have not yet taken up Spaak's suggestion, although there have been some recent moves in that direction. When they do, the present study will, I hope, help them to assess the alternatives and to evaluate the achievements, shortcomings and prospects of Atlantic parliamentary consultation as these appear after the first decade of experiment.

It is a pleasure to record my thanks to the friends and advisers who have given me the benefit of their knowledge and judgment. Their mention here does not of course imply endorsement of the book's conclusions nor, still less, complicity in its defects.

I am especially grateful to Professor Leland M. Goodrich and Professor Philip E. Mosely of Columbia University, who gave me helpful counsel at every stage. I should like to thank also Bryce Wood of the Social Science Research Council for much encouragement tempered by some ruthless editing.

Others to whom I am particularly indebted for comments and suggestions include Professors Roger Hilsman, Jr., René Albrecht-Carrié and Rudolph Binion of Columbia University;

Senator Jacob K. Javits; Congressman Wayne L. Hays; Sir Geoffrey de Freitas, K.C.M.G., M.P.; Lucien Radoux, M.P., Belgium; George S. Franklin, Jr. and Harold van B. Cleveland of the Council on Foreign Relations; Philander P. Claxton, Jr. and George Kaplan of the Department of State; Leonard B. Tennyson, Mrs. Alma Dauman and Mrs. Ella Krucoff of the European Community's Washington Information Service; Ben T. Moore of the Twentieth Century Fund; Julian S. Stein, Jr. of Washington; James R. Huntley then of the Atlantic Institute; Joseph Harned of the Atlantic Institute; and J.-M. Le Breton then of the staff of the Assembly of Western European Union.

Finally, I am greatly obliged to the officers and directors of the Atlantic Council of the United States and the Atlantic Institute for support in this undertaking, and to the Ford Foundation for a grant enabling me to pursue the subject in Europe.

A. H.

Washington, D. C.
September, 1966

CONTENTS

LIST OF TABLES

The Superparliaments

CHAPTER 1 INTERPARLIAMENTARY CONSULTATION
AND
ATLANTIC COOPERATION

International parliamentary consultative assemblies, of which the Atlantic area now has six, are one of the principal postwar innovations in regional organization. They were conceived variously as devices to stimulate, legitimize or supervise intergovernmental cooperation and integration. Their most enthusiastic proponents were those who saw in one or another of them the prefiguration of a European, Atlantic or world parliament endowed, in the wistful expression of the first such body, with "limited functions but real powers."[1] Their most emphatic opponents were those — primarily government officials — who saw them by the same token as threats to national sovereignty, hotbeds of irresponsible criticism or dangerous experiments in popular diplomacy. Both the fondest hopes and the worst fears have largely subsided in the light of some seventeen years' experience with the realities of the phenomenon.

The six assemblies, in order of their historical appearance, are:

(1) Consultative Assembly of the Council of Europe — 17 member states, 144 delegates (1949)

(2) Nordic Council — 4 member states, 53 delegates (1953)

(3) Western European Union Assembly — 7 member states, 89 delegates (1954)

(4) NATO Parliamentarians' Conference — 15 member states, about 180 delegates — variable (1955)[2]

(5) Benelux Consultative Parliamentary Council — 3 member states, 49 delegates (1957)

---

[1] Council of Europe, Consultative Assembly, 1st Session, September 6, 1949, Doc. 87, p. 7.

[2] The NATO Parliamentarians' Conference is advisory but unofficial and technically not "consultative."

1

(6)   European Parliament of the European Community —
      6 member states, 142 delegates (1958). (Common
      Assembly predecessor — 1952)

Of the six, four bear directly on the problems of Atlantic
cooperation examined in the present study; two — the Nordic
and Benelux Councils — can be exempted from the present
examination by reason of their local character and more restricted objectives.

EMERGENCE AND NATURE OF THE
CONSULTATIVE FUNCTION

The first venture in international parliamentary consultation, the Consultative Assembly of the Council of Europe,
is now in its seventeenth year. Its establishment by treaty
grew out of a proposal drawn up at the Hague Congress of
1948 by the leaders of the nongovernmental European Movement. Although the authors of the plan generally favored the
establishment in Western Europe of a supranational community, their memorandum[3] to the governments acknowledged
in effect that progress toward that objective must depend upon
governmental actions rather than constitutional processes.
Their politically oriented draft laid the basis for a new kind
of international organization and set forth for it and its five
imitators the essential nature of the interparliamentary consultative function.

In brief, according to the memorandum, the Consultative
Assembly was to provide machinery — additional machinery
would have been more accurate — through which legislators
and electorates could be associated with official discussions
and commitments concerning European regional cooperation
and integration. The new assembly would be a source of
ideas and constructive criticism and a goad to action. It
would examine new proposals and sift the practicable from
the impracticable. Through the publicity its deliberations and
recommendations provoked, it would create a body of public
and parliamentary opinion that would be both well-informed

---

[3]Memorandum submitted by the European Movement to the Five-
Power Study Commission — November 23, 1948, in European Movement
and the Council of Europe (London: Hutchinson & Co., 1949), p. 54-55.

and well-disposed. The work of the parliamentarians would thus impart a powerful impulse to the movement for regional unification.

It has been reported that when this plan was first put before Ernest Bevin, then British Foreign Minister, he exclaimed, "I don't like it, I don't like it. When you open that Pandora's box, you will find it full of Trojan horses."[4] At bottom, the initial British apprehension was that in some sense the Assembly might come to legislate and might thus encroach on the prerogatives of Parliament. The present frustration of many of its original backers is that it has failed to do just that. By the end of its second year, it was clear that the first experiment in interparliamentary consultation would fall short of expectations on both sides of the Channel.

PROBLEMS OF EVALUATION

If time has largely dissipated the illusions, it has done surprisingly little to establish a consensus among either observers or participants as to the nature and extent of the contributions that the Consultative Assembly and similar regional bodies have made or are likely to make to the achievement of cooperation and integration. Praised by some onlookers as essential catalysts of progress, they are scorned by others as boondoggles and talking-shops.

The main difficulty in appraising their functions is that consultative assemblies are concerned with such important but intangible matters as the mutual education of legislators, the improvement of intergovernmental relations, the refinement of policies, the clarification of issues, the broadening of public consensus. Evaluating their performance scientifically would call for measuring the volume of public discussion attributable to each assembly, determining the extent to which parliamentarians' participation has modified their views of political issues, and drawing up a balance sheet that sets the roster of assembly recommendations against the corresponding actions taken by national governments.

---

[4]Quoted in Lord Strang, Home and Abroad (London: Andre Deutsch, 1956), p. 290.

For the most part, interparliamentary consultation does not lend itself to such quantitative analysis. The evidence is necessarily fragmentary and the judgments are ultimately subjective.[5] One is therefore free to conclude, with Theodore White, that the Consultative Assembly, for example, is a "nonsensical body" bearing no relation to the "real mechanics of European politics,"[6] or with André Philip that the Assembly has actually played a decisive role in the creation of the European Coal and Steel Community.[7] On the whole, however, the evidence considered in the present study suggests that interparliamentary consultation has certain distinct advantages as well as limitations and that neither the boondoggle — talking-shop thesis nor the essential-catalyst view provides an adequate appraisal.

Interparliamentary consultation is primarily a means by which members of national parliaments may be enabled to enhance their influence over and their support of certain intergovernmental agencies and activites. It is a useful if hardly revolutionary innovation in regional cooperation. There are some, mainly Atlantic or European "federalists," who believe that one or another of the regional parliamentary assemblies must eventually evolve into a supranational parliament with legislative powers. The present study, however, is concerned with the importance, the techniques and the prospects of strengthening and rationalizing interparliamentary consultation as a means of improving regional international relations. For this purpose the federalist proposition that the consultative assemblies are or ought to be embryonic legislatures is immaterial.

Similarly, while the present study is focused on Atlantic organization, there is no intention to suggest that progress in that regard must or should be at the expense of European unification. Indeed, as will be indicated below, there are

---

[5]The official Balance Sheet of the Work of the Council of Europe concedes the imponderables of evaluation and confines itself to listing resolutions adopted and reporting relevant subsequent developments — Publication of the Directorate of Information for 1949-1956 (Strasbourg: 1956).

[6]Theodore H. White, Fire in the Ashes: Europe in Mid-Century (New York: William Sloane Associates, 1953), p. 259.

[7]André Philip, L'Europe unie et sa place dans l'économie internationale (Paris: Presses universitaires de France, 1953), p. 314.

reasons for believing that more effective interparliamentary relations among all members of the OECD would strengthen those within the European Community who desire to see it achieve further integration while maintaining and developing external policies that are consistent with the interests of the Free World as a whole.

In this prospect lies one of the reasons for the conclusion that Atlantic interparliamentary consultation serves the American interest as well as that of other free countries. It was in part on such reasoning that, unlike most other foreign offices concerned, the U. S. Department of State gave its cordial if unostentatious backing to the establishment of the NATO Parliamentarians' Conference a decade ago and later encouraged the efforts of certain Congressional leaders to establish a consultative Atlantic Assembly. Such a policy assumes that the organization of certain Atlantic nations for cooperation in military defense and economic growth has proved and remains important. And it represents an evaluation, which the experience of the past seventeen years tends to confirm, that interparliamentary consultation can contribute new ideas, constructive criticism or political support to the intergovernmental activities in those fields. To the extent that this is true, it is clear that the U. S. interest would be served by arrangements permitting the full participation of North American as well as Western European legislators.

RESOLUTIONS—CLASSIFICATION AND CRITERIA

If the value of international parliamentary assemblies had to depend solely on the quality and efficacy of their formal resolutions, none perhaps could look forward to an assured future. Their publicists and partisans rightly insist on such additional values as the personal contacts among influential leaders, the informal exchanges of information and opinion, and the stimulus the discussions give to consideration of major issues by press and public.

An assembly can, however, approach optimum performance only if its reports and recommendations perform one or more of three functions. These are to propose or inspire timely new solutions or projects; to promote, through review and criticism, the better execution of existing policies and programs; and to develop more solid parliamentary and public support for the institutions and the purposes they serve.

One of the special advantages of an international consultative assembly is that it provides a pertinent but different vantage point from which legislative leaders can view their international responsibilities. Another is that it gives participants a firsthand acquaintance with the preoccupations of their foreign colleagues on matters of common interest. It is natural and salutary that they find themselves working toward wider areas of international agreement, and the process has provided a valuable new source of policy formation.[8]

The experience of the assemblies to date suggests, however, that their success in the field of policy formation is dependent on the observance of two cardinal principles. One, applicable to the assemblies themselves, is that the importance of the results is directly proportionate to the concreteness and relevance of resolutions and to the thoroughness of the study and investigation that precedes their drafting. The other principle, applicable to the executive agencies, is that consultative assemblies should be consulted. Both of these basic and interacting propositions have often been enunciated by participants in the various assemblies. Both have been liberally disregarded.

In the aggregate, assembly resolutions fall into three broad categories that may perhaps be designated as procedural, declarative and operative.

Procedural resolutions are of course those relating to the internal organization and methods of the assembly. They provide an important key to the evolution of the consultative technique.

---

[8]Cf. Philip, ibid., p. 314-315: "Finally, the Strasbourg discussions have been an element in the maturing of the European political idea. After the first shocks among national delegates having different temperaments and diverse parliamentary customs, a veritable parliamentary community was constituted, and the members felt themselves divided much less by their nationalities than by their various political, economic and social tendencies. And above all, very quickly, the real nature of the European problem became clear [i.e., the opposing conceptions of Britain and the Six]."

Declarative resolutions, typically, reaffirm the faith of the organization in Western values, or proclaim the determination of the West to defend itself, preserve the peace, promote human freedom and provide for the general welfare. They are by nature unoriginal, rhetorical and repetitive. It would, however, be a mistake to dismiss them as necessarily superfluous. They usually arise out of current issues in East-West diplomacy that are of such fundamental importance that no international forgathering of elected representatives could fail to go on record about them. If on the whole such resolutions do not noticeably affect the struggle for men's minds, it is at least arguable that a cumulative silence on such matters on the part of a body of Western parliamentarians would encourage dangerous misapprehensions.

Operative resolutions are those intended to stimulate action — to modify policies, improve procedures, initiate programs or strengthen institutions. It is the implicit assumption of such resolutions that an international parliamentary body can bring to bear on international problems some new insight or some increment of the "political will" necessary to resolve them.

Here indeed is the underlying rationale of a consultative assembly. But the reality and significance of the "political will" to be manifested is, again, directly proportionate to the concreteness of the proposal. All too frequently the participants, conscious of the setting in which they are for the moment deliberating, and aware that Western cooperation is plagued with serious shortcomings, propose and adopt resolutions that are long on good will and short on specifications. Such resolutions can usually be identified by their reliance on a small number of sonorous and overworked transitive verbs: "coordinate," "intensify," "strengthen," "accelerate," "improve," "harmonize," "centralize," "expand." The other device of resolutions that may be said to show the will but not the way is of course to propose a conference, study, survey, investigation, inventory or review, the utility of which is to be assured by the appointment of appropriate, selected or qualified specialists with a mandate to be exhaustive, comprehensive, intensive or systematic.

The best of the operative resolutions constitute the core of a consultative assembly's achievement. The worst of the operative resolutions are apt to be merely inoperative.

MOBILIZATION OF PARLIAMENTARY PRESSURE

Since all resolutions of a consultative assembly are by definition advisory, their ultimate translation into action is likely to depend on something more than their timeliness and other intrinsic merits. The required additive is the collective and individual influence that the participants are able to exert upon the national governments and the executive agencies. How to obtain a wider and more attentive hearing for their resolutions is the greatest single problem and a major preoccupation of the consultative assemblies. One approach, which presupposes an assembly's official status, is to impose upon the related executive agencies a statutory obligation to report on actions taken to implement the recommendations. Another is to endow the assembly with some carefully defined power of disagreement or censure. There has been, in fact, a multiplicity of efforts in this domain, ranging from the assertion of an assembly's independence in determining its own agenda to the establishment of a permanent committee to organize systematic "follow-up" procedures at the national level. The techniques evolved and the results obtained by the Consultative Assembly of the Council of Europe are particularly noteworthy.

No combination of such devices, however, can be expected to revolutionize the record of measurable results. The only reliable answer to the problem of implementation is legislative power. The idea of an Atlantic legislature is not without its advocates, but it presupposes a supranational community with a common executive, which is at best a long step from the present situation. It is conceivable, as a recent study puts it, that "as the Atlantic Community is slowly being built, the historic struggle between executive and legislative power which characterized the evolution of Western democratic government will be re-enacted, almost unconsciously, on a regional scale."[9] That process — or more accurately, the peaceful extension of the governmental function to the regional plane — will require the development of a sense of community that has proved elusive even among the Six of "Little Europe." Meanwhile, within the existing framework of Atlantic relations,

---

[9]Robert Strausz-Hupé, James E. Dougherty and William R. Kintner, Building the Atlantic World (New York: Harper & Row, 1963), p. 289.

there are substantial theoretical possibilities for making interparliamentary consultation more effective, and so, perhaps, for assisting the emergence of that "true Atlantic Community" which at least one distinguished Atlantic group has proclaimed attainable by 1972.[10]

RATIONALIZATION OF THE CONSULTATIVE PROCESS

If, as has been suggested, evaluations of the consultative process are necessarily tentative, there are other aspects of the phenomenon about which it is possible and, in the light of recent developments, desirable to be more dogmatic. In the aggregate the present six assemblies are in session about one-fourth of each year, not counting the work of their committees, in which much of the work is done. They claim the time of more than 500 national legislators of twenty Western countries both during and between sessions. They employ about a thousand international civil servants, in addition to enlisting the part-time attention of countless others in the national governments and in a variety of international organizations. Their aggregate annual budgets come to some $10 million. In varying degrees they overlap in purpose, powers, method and membership.

A long-felt concern over unhealthy proliferation, with its attendant disadvantages of duplicated effort, overburdening of legislators and confusion of public opinion, has led neither to a rationalization of the existing array of assemblies nor to a moratorium on proposals to create others. Some of the current proposals, to be sure, contemplate the dissolution or consolidation of certain existing assemblies. The experience of the past seventeen years, however, has shown that it is easier to establish a parliamentary assembly than to make one disappear. This goes deeper than the matter of institutional inertia, although that provides a part of the explanation. The six assemblies were created at different historical conjunctures, to meet different problems among different groupings of states and to do so by different methods. Arguably, at least, as Kenneth Lindsay observed in 1960, "They cannot be

---

[10] The officially sponsored Atlantic Convention of NATO Nations, "Declaration of Paris," in U. S. Citizens Commission on NATO, Report to Congress, House Document No. 433, June 18, 1962, p. 9.

rationalized away by any quasi-logical paper schemes, because they are tied to specific regional, functional and even structural methods of international co-operation."[11]

One proposal for a new parliamentary assembly that has lately engaged the serious attention of Western parliamentarians and some of their governments does contemplate the merger or disappearance of at least three of the six existing bodies. That proposal was initiated by the Atlantic Convention of NATO Nations in January 1962 and was approved in principle by the eighth annual NATO Parliamentarians' Conference (NPC) in November of that year. The resolution of the Conference proposed in essence the "evolution" of existing entities into two international parliamentary bodies — "one a Parliament for a United Europe and the other an Assembly for the Atlantic Partnership."[12] The NPC established a special subcommittee "to study and submit recommendations" to the 1963 session on "a constitution or charter for a consultative Atlantic Assembly" that would serve "as a single consultative parliamentary body both for the North Atlantic Treaty Organisation and for the Organisation for Economic Co-operation and Development. . . ."[13]

Events of the ensuing year led the NATO parliamentarians in November 1963 to conclude that the project had become "impractical for the present."[14] The new and temporarily insuperable obstacles were, as the Political Committee explained, "the apparent foreclosure for the time being of the possibility of an expanded European Economic Community, and, more important perhaps, the prevailing uncertainty on the part of some members of the Alliance with respect to the

---

[11]Kenneth Lindsay, European Assemblies: The Experimental Period, 1949-1959 (London: Stevens & Sons, Ltd., 1960), p. 5.

[12]NATO Parliamentarians' Conference (NPC), 8th Session, Reports and Recommendations, November 1962, p. 47. See also Atlantic Convention of NATO Nations, Declaration of Paris, January 19, 1962, p. 4-6.

[13]Ibid., p. 47-48.

[14]NPC, Report of the Political Committee, F. 126, Rev. 3, 9th Annual Session, November 4-9, 1963, p. 1. Both the idea of establishing a consultative Atlantic Assembly and the idea of giving the NPC official consultative status were rejected. The political factors affecting the possibilities of interparliamentary reorganization are reviewed in Chapter 9.

aims and intentions of other members of the Alliance." The Committee made it clear, however, that the project for a consultative Atlantic Assembly is to be viewed as an important piece of unfinished business. The NPC's "aspirations are unaltered," as is its conviction that "the eventual creation of such an Assembly, with formal status and consultative powers, would be a major, dramatic step toward Atlantic solidarity."[15]

The NATO parliamentarians' 1962 project was in fact a natural outgrowth of a shift in trans-Atlantic relationships that had already been reflected in formal acts of the governments concerned. By 1960 leaders on both sides of the Atlantic had concluded that Western Europe, which had recovered from the effects of the war and was taking phenomenal strides toward opulence and unity, should begin to assume the privileges and responsibilities of full "partnership" with North America. Moreover, as thoughtful advocates of European integration had generally anticipated, the emergence of a European Community was beginning to present new problems as well as new opportunities and was putting some of the chronic issues in a different light. The establishment of the OECD was the first major step toward strengthening the machinery of trans-Atlantic collaboration. The proposal for an Atlantic Assembly was conceived to be another.[16]

The emergence of the proposal for a consultative Atlantic Assembly as a genuine if relatively low-keyed political issue has compelled its advocates and its critics alike to consider three broad questions: Is such an assembly politically attainable? How should it be organized? What difference would it make?

---

[15]Ibid., p. 3. The Special Committee, whose report became the basis for the decision to defer attempts to establish a consultative assembly, was more dubious. It declared that even if the project should later appear feasible, "it is not certain that our favor and support should be given to consultative [i.e., official] status." — Report (F 125, Rev. 2), November 1963, p. 5.

[16]Others worth noting are those of Pierre Uri in Partnership for Progress: A Program for Transatlantic Action (New York: Harper and Row, for the Atlantic Institute, 1963), p. 96-107. See also recommendations of the NATO Parliamentarians' Conference and the Atlantic Convention of NATO Nations (op. cit.).

The present study deals essentially with the latter two questions. For the reasons indicated, it remains necessary to suspend judgment on the question of practicability. Even if that were not the case, there is at this juncture something to be gained from an attempt to isolate the institutional from the political factors and to determine theoretically what set of international arrangements might most effectively associate Atlantic parliamentarians with the processes of Atlantic cooperation. Accordingly, the present study undertakes to examine the manner in which organized international parliamentary activity has sought to influence Atlantic regional developments, and to appraise the achievements and shortcomings of such activity to date. It seeks on that basis to suggest what modifications of structure, status, methods and functions might be expected to make interparliamentary consultation more productive.

CHAPTER **2** THE NATO
PARLIAMENTARIANS' CONFERENCE—
ORIGINS AND PROCEDURES

In addition to the NATO Parliamentarians' Conference, established in 1955, annual encounters between American and foreign legislators occur through the sessions of the Commonwealth Parliamentarians Association, which U. S. delegations attend as observers, the Inter-Parliamentary Union (since 1889) and its American Republics Branch, the Canada-United States Interparliamentary Group (since 1959), and the Mexico-United States Interparliamentary Group (since 1961). Other contacts are arranged occasionally on a bilateral basis.

ORIGINS AND ESTABLISHMENT

The first formal trans-Atlantic parliamentary conference was held at Strasbourg in November 1951 on the initiative of the Council of Europe; it brought fourteen U. S. Senators and Representatives together with a twenty-member delegation from the Consultative Assembly. The meeting of 1951, which was called to discuss "The Union of Europe: its progress, problems and place in the Western World," generated considerably more controversy than has developed thus far in the deliberations of the NPC. Its value lay primarily in the mutual education of its participants. Lord Layton later told the Consultative Assembly:

The first inter-continental parliamentary debate is over. . . . We have learned where certain misconceptions lie and we must do our best to remove them. It is even more important that we should have had the rare privilege of seeing ourselves as others see us. . . . The Americans are right to be impatient. . . . The fresh breeze from the West which blew through this hall last week should stimulate us to fresh efforts and so justify the confidence of President Truman, who expressed the opinion to me last June that a conference between the parliamentarians of Europe and America could do nothing but good.[1]

Proposals for a specifically Atlantic consultative assembly date from about that time, although efforts by Guy Mollet as President of the Strasbourg Assembly to organize subsequent encounters of this sort gained little support at the time from U. S. legislators.[2] Interest in proposals for an Atlantic assembly was further stimulated some two years later with the appearance of the Coal–Steel Community's "supranational" assembly and the announcement of official plans for a six-nation European Political Authority. These European developments raised the possibility, as Patrick Gordon Walker put it, that "the Council of Europe is in danger of atrophy through having its lifeblood drawn off into other organizations."[3] Suggestions were not lacking that in that event it ought to be replaced by a wider grouping. As the London Economist suggested, "Once European federation begins in earnest, an Atlantic and not a purely European framework will be needed to keep the policies and development of the new federal unit in line with the interests of the free world."[4]

The first NATO Parliamentarians' Conference was held at NATO headquarters in the Palais de Chaillot July 18 to 23, 1955, with some 200 parliamentarians present from the fifteen NATO countries. The invitations, which were addressed by the Speaker of the Canadian Senate, Wishart

[1] Council of Europe, Consultative Assembly, Official Report of Debates, November 27, 1951, p. 481. See also: Council of Europe, Conference of Strasbourg between Delegations of the Congress of the United States of America and of the Consultative Assembly of the Council of Europe, Official Record of Debates (Strasbourg: November 19–23, 1951).

[2] Such proposals included those of Lord Layton in European and Atlantic Digest (London: April 1952), p. 40–42; Senator Gillette in a speech of November 20, 1951, cited in American Committee on United Europe, Report from Strasbourg (New York: January 1953), p. 23. Cf. Freedom and Union, January 1952 (Washington: Federal Union, Inc.), p. 4; Geoffrey de Freitas' Introduction in The North Atlantic Treaty Organization Parliamentarians' Conference 1955–1959 (London: The Hansard Society for Parliamentary Government, 1960), p. 3; and Livingston Hartley, "A North Atlantic Assembly: Its Purpose, Function and Structure," Freedom and Union, Washington: January 1953, p. 1.

[3] Council of Europe, 4th Session, op. cit., September 16, 1952, p. 311.

[4] September 20, 1952, p. 672.

McLean Robertson, to his counterparts of the other national legislatures, grew out of a series of preliminary discussions in which Norwegian and Canadian M.P.'s — notably Finn Moe and Robertson — played a leading part. As with the Council of Europe, which came into being through the exertions of the European Movement, the establishment of the NPC owed much to the impetus and assistance provided by an international citizens organization, in this case the Sponsors of the Declaration of Atlantic Unity.

The establishment of the Conference was, in the words of Geoffrey de Freitas, one of its founders, "the final step in the long campaign of a few parliamentarians to get their governments interested in a forum for discussing problems of the Atlantic community."[5] With the exception of the U. S. State Department, there was at the time little encouragement from the foreign offices, whose reservations about augmenting opportunities for parliamentary interference in general were reinforced by concern for the security of NATO's military information in particular. The NPC therefore came into being under exclusively parliamentary sponsorship, unencumbered by official responsibility or status.

INTERNAL ARRANGEMENTS

Sessions

The NATO Parliamentarians' Conference meets annually in November for an average of five and a half days. Except for the Fifth Session, which was convened in Washington, and the Eleventh, which met in New York, all sessions have been held in Paris at the NATO Headquarters. The dates of each session are set by the Standing Committee.

Selection of Participants

The Speakers of the national parliaments determine the list of participants in consultation with the leaders of the

---

[5] de Freitas, op. cit., p. 3. Cf. letter by Walden Moore, Director of Declaration of Atlantic Unity, to Lord Crathorne, May 6, 1963, on establishment of the Conference. The Declaration helped develop interest in the project among legislators in North America and Europe and sponsored meetings for them at which plans were evolved.

principal non-Communist political parties. There is no limit
to the number of participants each country may send, beyond
the requirement that representatives must be members of the
national parliaments of the NATO countries. The method of
their selection tends to give the Conference greater moral
authority than might otherwise be the case. At the first
session, in 1955, the Conference rejected a Canadian proposal
that "interested Parliamentarians" in each country organize
national NATO Parliamentary Associations which could then
be combined and coordinated through a "NATO Inter-Parliamentary Association with its Headquarters and Secretariat
at Paris." In rejecting this formula, the Conference deliberately sought to assure that members would not be
"merely enthusiasts."[6] Thus as one observer has noted,
". . . The element of crankiness sometimes found in voluntary and quasi-official organisations is largely eliminated.
Delegations are not necessarily selected because they have
shown an active interest in NATO, and it is not unusual for
them to show a critical approach to its activities. Such a
means of selection has the effect of keeping the feet of the
Conference firmly on the ground, both with regard to its
recommendations and its budget."[7]

Conference Services and Staff

Although the NATO Secretary General was on record by
late 1954 in favor of an occasional "combined meeting" of
NATO M.P. associations and had offered to "place all facilities
at their disposal,"[8] the NPC's conference and secretarial
arrangements were and largely remain modest and makeshift.
In the early years, according to the organization's second
Treasurer, "So little help was forthcoming from the staff at
NATO Headquarters that my own private secretary served
the international Standing Committee and many of the trans-
lations were done by friends from the Secretariat of the

[6]NPC Secretariat, A Summary of the Meeting of Members of Parliament from NATO Countries, 1st Session, July 18-22, 1955, p. 9-11. The
German Social Democrats attended for the first time in the Sixth Session — See Verbatim Report, 24th November 1960 (a.m.), p. 37.

[7]European Organisations (London: Political and Economic Planning,
1959), p. 204.

[8]Lord Ismay, NATO: The First Five Years, 1949-1954 (Netherlands:
Bosch-Utrecht, 1954), p. 157.

Council of Europe who had come to the Palais de Chaillot as spectators."[9] The first conference was held without the assistance of any permanent NPC staff and it was not until January 1956 that a one-room secretariat was opened in London, by Douglas Robinson, the first Executive Secretary, with a staff that has since varied in number from two to twelve. The headquarters was transferred to Paris in June 1960, shortly after its direction was assumed by Otto van H. Labberton of the Netherlands.[10]

Budget

The NPC's first annual budget (July 1955 to June 1956) amounted to £4,047. It was increased to £40,000 or some $112,000 in January 1958, when the organization adopted a calendar financial year, and stands today at only about $220,000. National contributions are made in accordance with the NATO cost-sharing formula.[11] Notwithstanding the modest scale of its budgetary demands, the NPC has been plagued with delays in payments from legislative or foreign office funds. The continued reliance on such minimal housekeeping arrangements has been the subject of growing dissatisfaction on the part of NPC participants.

Aims and Methods

The formal statement of NPC aims is broad and brief: "The Conference, by virtue of its membership, drawn from the various national parliaments, provides an informal link between the responsible NATO authorities and these parliaments. Through its discussions, it helps to promote a common

---

[9]G. de Freitas, op. cit., p. 4.

[10]The Secretariat, now numbering a half dozen, is located at 12 rue du Bois de Boulogne, Neuilly-sur-Seine, France.

[11]The NATO cost-sharing formula is as follows:

Belgium	2.86%	Greece	0.39%	Norway	1.15%
Canada	5.80	Iceland	0.05	Portugal	0.65
Denmark	1.65	Italy	5.96	Turkey	1.65
France	17.10	Luxembourg	0.09	United Kingdom	19.50
Germany	16.10	Netherlands	2.85	United States	24.20

feeling of Atlantic solidarity in the various legislative
assemblies and to further the aims of the Atlantic Alliance."[12]

The Conference has sought to serve those aims through
a program that has to date been conducted with a minimum
of formality. Reports and recommendations are adopted in
final plenary meetings and published and distributed by the
Secretariat to appropriate national and international
agencies.[13] The Conference has addressed its resolutions
explicitly to the North Atlantic Council, the NATO Secretary
General, the OECD, the collective national parliaments, the
collective member governments and private agencies — freely
prefacing the operative clauses with such terms as: "calls
upon," "invites," "requests," "recommends," "reminds,"
"emphasizes," "reiterates," "regrets," "welcomes," "com-
mends" and "expects." Other resolutions, in the nature of
declarations of principle, have been aimed at the Communist
bloc or the world at large.

Structure—Committees

Article 23 of the NPC Rules of Procedure provides for
the establishment of committees to deal respectively with
political and military affairs and with "matters arising under
Article 2 of the North Atlantic Treaty." It further stipulates
that "if possible" each committee shall have "at least one
member from each delegation." Two additional committees
were established later, and the present committee structure
is as follows: Political Committee, Military Committee,
Economic Committee, Scientific and Technical Committee,
Cultural Affairs and Information Committee.

In addition, the Conference elects annually a Standing
Committee (Articles 9 and 10) comprising one member and
a deputy from each delegation including the four Vice Presidents, plus the President and Treasurer ex officio. The
Standing Committee handles Conference business between

---

[12]NPC, Rules of Procedure (Paris: November 1961), p. i.

[13]Article 7 provides that "The President shall forward copies of
all recommendations and/or resolutions adopted by the conference to
the NATO Council and to the presiding officers of national parliaments
in member countries."

sessions, prepares the agenda and budgets and has the important duty "to take all possible steps through the NATO Council and by other appropriate methods to secure the adoption of the Recommendations and/or Resolutions of the Conference."

In 1961, in the wake of criticism about the excessive number of resolutions, the NPC established a Drafting Committee. It screens and may advise the cutting, combining or other editing of all resolutions. The Drafting Committee consists of the members of the Standing Committee plus the Chairman and Rapporteur of the substantive committee concerned.

Finally, the Bureau, comprising the President of the Conference, a First Vice President, three additional Vice Presidents and the Treasurer, is charged (Article 8) with the appointment of the Executive Secretary and with general supervision of the staff.

Conduct of Business

Plenary sessions are held in a large committee room. Delegates are grouped by country around a single large table. Plenary meetings are devoted to the discussion and voting of committee recommendations and to speeches by key NATO and government officials who are invited by the Conference to report on the affairs of the Alliance. The guest speakers have generally delivered themselves of pertinent and informative reports. Many of them, moreover, have submitted to questioning, on or off the record, by the parliamentarians. There is little doubt that the guest performances have been among the highlights of the sessions.[14]

Typically, the first day and a half is devoted to plenary meetings, at which guest speakers are heard and some debate

---

[14]Guest participants have included: NATO Secretary General Lord Ismay, General Alfred N. Gruenther, Field Marshall Montgomery, Secretary of State Christian A. Herter, Admiral Jerauld Wright, Dean Acheson, NATO Secretary General P.-H. Spaak, Vice President-elect Lyndon Johnson, General Lauris Norstad, French Premier Michel Debré, Norwegian Foreign Minister Halvard Lange, Foreign Minister Couve de Murville, NATO Secretary General Dirk U. Stikker, U. S. Secretary of the Army Elvis I. Stahr, EEC Commission Chairman Walter Hallstein, Under Secretary of State George Ball, NATO Secretary General Manlio Brosio, and Vice President Hubert H. Humphrey.

may be held. This is followed by approximately two days of committee meetings, which "shall not be held in public" (Article 27-1), although "observers" may attend on invitation of the chairman (Article 27-4). Since the Second Session, all resolutions originate in committees. A final day and a half of plenary meetings is taken to elect officers and to discuss and vote the committee reports.

Voting

The procedure in plenary session for the adoption of recommendations differs from that of the European assemblies and reflects the less formal and less controversial character of the deliberations to date. NPC participants are seated by national delegations and vote as a unit. Votes are weighted in such a way that each European delegation has the same number of votes as it has in the Consultative Assembly of the Council of Europe and the United States has exactly twice the voting strength of each of the European "big four." The breakdown as adopted by the Standing Committee in February 1956 is as follows:

Table 1
National Voting Weights in NPC

	Votes in Plenary	Votes in Committee
United States	36	10
United Kingdom France Germany Italy	18 each	5 each
Canada	12	3
Turkey	10	3
Belgium Greece Netherlands	7 each	2 each
Denmark Norway Portugal	5 each	2 each
Iceland Luxembourg	3 each	1 each
TOTALS. . . .	172	50

According to Article 22-1, "A recommendation or resolution shall be carried if supported by two-thirds of the votes cast, provided those two-thirds represent at least half the total number of delegates[15] to the Conference." In fact virtually all measures have carried unanimously or with a few abstentions.

Voting in committees is by "absolute majority of the votes cast" (Article 28-2) but resolutions or recommendations cannot be adopted by a committee "unless at least half its members are present" (Article 27-3).

Conference and committee officers, including members of the Standing Committee, are elected annually by majority vote and are eligible for re-election (Articles 1, 2, 3 and 25). There is however a tradition favoring the annual rotation of the Presidency.[16]

CONCLUSIONS

The procedures of the NPC as set forth in the Rules of November 1961 contain some anomalies, ambiguities and inconsistencies and will undoubtedly require overhauling if the Assembly should gain official status or take on important new functions. Perhaps most noteworthy is the unit-voting rule which could have the undesirable effect of preventing the emergence of inter-party or individual differences. This rule is difficult to reconcile logically with Article 21, which stipulates that "Delegates speak and act on their own responsibility, and their statements are not binding on their governments, parliaments or parties."

It will also become important, in the event that the Conference assumes official functions, to develop more adequate conference records. At present mimeographed verbatim

---

[15]Sic. A comparison with the French text indicates that the requisite majority must represent at least half the total number of votes, i.e., one-half of 172, rather than one-half the number of delegates, which is of course variable and unpredictable.

[16]See NPC, Meeting of the Standing Committee, London, September 9, 1958, Appendix IV.

reports (of varying quality) of the plenary meetings are published, as required in Article 31. Even these, however, have not been distributed to all participants on a regular basis, and in the 8th Session (1962), Senator Karl E. Mundt urged that arrangements be made to correct this.[17] There is no clear requirement regarding committee documents; in too many cases no record of committee discussions is available, other than what may be reflected in the Rapporteur's report accompanying draft resolutions. The official languages are English and French and the verbatim records of plenary meetings carry the delegates' interventions in one or the other but not both.

Pending further consideration of the more substantial reforms contemplated in 1962, the Conference adopted unanimously, in 1963, a number of recommendations of its Special, Standing and Political committees that look to modest improvements in efficiency. These decisions provided that the Committee chairmen should become members ex officio of the Standing Committee in an advisory capacity; that as from January 1, 1965, the Conference shall meet twice a year, in the fall and spring, preferably alternately in Europe and North America; that a Rapporteur General shall be appointed "to keep the Conference and all Committees of the Conference continually informed of the work in progress and to prepare an annual summary and report of the work of the Conference and of all the problems concerning NATO itself"; and finally, that the Executive Secretary be empowered to recruit two additional assistants and two additional secretaries "and any other ancillary staff which may be needed to assist in carrying out the above reforms."[18]

Partly because funds are insufficient, these decisions have not yet been fully implemented. The Conference adopted a proposal by the Standing Committee to increase the budget for 1965 by an unstipulated amount to cover the proposed increase of staff.[19] The delay of a year was designed, as the

---

[17]NPC, Verbatim Report, 8th Session, November 16, a.m., 1962, p. 42.

[18]NPC, Report of the Political Committee, 9th Annual Session (F. 188), November 1963, p. 2; voted November 8, p.m., 1963, p. 51.

[19]Resolution ibid., 2d Verbatim Report, 2d Plenary Session, November 7, a.m., 1963, p. 9; voted November 8, p.m., 1963, p. 51.

President explained, to give the Standing Committee time to determine "the money we can extract from national governments."[20] Meanwhile, a 5 percent budget increase was authorized for 1964 to cover salary and other cost increases.[21]

Only the existence of a strong consensus on most of the important questions has prevented the NPC's budgetary and staff restrictions, its loosely drafted Rules of Procedure and its casual management of record-keeping from causing difficulties. Any revision of methods and procedures, however, should be prepared in the light of whatever new functions and structure the organization may acquire.

---

[20]Ibid., p. 57.

[21]Ibid.

3

THE NATO PARLIAMENTARIANS' CONFERENCE — POLICIES AND PROBLEMS

In its eleven annual sessions to date, the NATO Parliamentarians' Conference has adopted some 200 resolutions. These have ranged in subject matter from regional political consultation, peaceful settlement of disputes, military command reorganization, equipment standardization, development assistance and disarmament to early manufactures, exotic language study, saline water conversion and control of pharmaceutical toxicity.

SUBSTANTIVE PROGRAM

Over the past eight years (the first three representing a less typical period of "running-in," in which few resolutions were adopted), the Conference turned out an average of nearly 24 resolutions per session. On the basis of the somewhat arbitrary but useful classification suggested in the first chapter, about two-thirds of these were declarative. Only a fourth or less appeared classifiable as operative. The output has tended to level off at about 20 resolutions per session from the peak of 32 in 1959, and in recent sessions there has been a notable increase in the ratio of operative to declarative resolutions. It is too early to determine whether this represents a continuing pattern, although the statements of many participants tend to confirm a growing desire to see the Conference select fewer problems and deal with them more concretely.[1]

---

[1]Cf. NPC Report of Special Committee, 9th Session, November 4-9, 1963, p. 3. "International parliamentary experience of about ten years," Colonel J. J. Fens (Netherlands) has remarked, "has taught me that it is easier to get the ear of international Councils of Ministers and national governments by only a few well-drafted resolutions or recommendations, than by a shower of wide-spoken considerations, sermons and meditations." --NPC, Verbatim Report, 6th Session, November 25, 1960, p.m., p. 27. The same point was emphasized by Secretary General Spaak in his address to the Fifth Session. Commenting on the difficulties

Another factor in the relative decline in the number of purely declarative resolutions is that on several issues — Berlin and disarmament, for example — the Conference has not found much to add to its original thoughts, and the participants' interest in annual repetition has perhaps begun to pall. The trend, if such it is, deserves encouragement, and could perhaps be fostered by the practice of deciding on occasion that a given issue might usefully be studied and debated without being made the subject of a formal resolution. In many instances the statements of individual parliamentarians are far more significant on a particular issue than the bland generality that emerges from the need to adopt a resolution about it.[2]

Military Committee

It is noteworthy that in an assembly whose main focus is the Atlantic Alliance, one of the least prolific of the permanent committees has been the Military Committee. Over the entire period, it has presented 30 resolutions, many of them repetitious, as against 54 for the Political Committee, 46 for the Economic Committee, 36 for the Scientific and Cultural Committee (and 24 for the Cultural Affairs and Information Committee).

Military problems are more technical than most of the issues treated by the other committees, and security considerations add to the normal difficulties of parliamentarians

---

of getting large sums from governments for cultural and scientific projects, he said, ". . . But experience has taught me that if one presents to the governments projects that have been carefully studied, that are practical and that respond to precise necessities, the governments will show the necessary good will. . . ."--Ibid.,5th Session, November 19, 1959, p.m., p. 110. Cf. Vice President Hubert H. Humphrey: "Consultation will be effective in the degree that it looks to action and not merely talk."--- speech before the NATO Parliamentarians' Conference, 11th Session, New York, October 5, 1965.

[2]A case in point was the debate in the 9th Session concerning the proposed Multilateral Force. Diametrically opposed and strongly held views, especially between French and U. S. delegates, were "compromised" in a resolution noting that control of nuclear weapons is a political question and recommending that it be debated in the national parliaments and in ensuing NPC sessions. -- Op. cit., Reports, Resolutions and Recommendations, 1963; Verbatim Report, November 7, p.m., 1963, p. 42-62.

in developing relevant information and acquiring the sort of
expertise that would lend greater authority to Conference
pronouncements in this field. The Military Committee inevitably has been less wide-ranging and less inventive in its
recommendations than some of the others. Nor has it undertaken the sort of studies and reports that have, as will be
seen in Chapter 4, enhanced the importance of the Assembly
of Western European Union. The main thrust of the NPC
Military Committee has been to urge more rapid and more
adequate performance on the part of the NATO partners with
regard to announced official goals and projects and to deplore
the chronic failure of governments and Council to attain
either a more rational degree of integration in defense
preparation or a closer approximation of the accepted minimum force levels.

The first report of the Military Committee, presented to
the second session, indicated that it was "reluctant to make
definite statements, partly for lack of information, but partly
also because, with the NATO shield not yet completed, it
seemed unrealistic to set up new objectives."[3] In the third
session the Conference, on the committee's advice, advocated
closer coordination in matters of logistics, organization and
communication and proposed "adequate strategic reprisal
forces and sufficient ground, air and naval forces."[4] In the
fourth session, the committee urged "more frequent and regular meetings of Defense Ministers," and asserted that "the
ground forces of NATO should be, as a matter of absolute
priority, brought up to the minimum requirements as laid
down by the North Atlantic Council." It also recommended
"high priority" for "the future standardization of logistics
systems, organization, armament and equipment" and proposed that the Brussels Treaty "be amended in order to allow
Germany to build coastal anti-submarine craft necessary to
fulfill the task that has been allotted to it."[5]

This pattern of recommendation has been substantially
followed in subsequent sessions, with certain variations to
include support for the Mobile Force, a strengthening of naval

---

[3]Reported in de Freitas, op. cit., p. 18.

[4]NPC, op. cit., 3d Session, November 11-16, 1957, p. 23.

[5]U.S. Senate, Fourth NATO Parliamentarians' Conference (November
15-21, 1958), 86th Congress, 1st Session, January 15, 1959, p. 8.

forces, establishment of a NATO "food and raw materials bank" and the development of a common system of air defense and detection.

One military resolution, in the fifth session, introduced a promising note of exasperation. It declared that, "This Committee and this Conference have repeatedly put forward resolutions to the Council deploring the shortfall in the ground forces of the shield below the minimum requirements laid out by the Council itself." Further, the Conference "deplores the failure of the Council of Ministers of NATO, despite repeated requests from this Conference, to effect standardisation of supply lines, weapons and equipment of the shield forces" and declared that "the permanent representatives of the North Atlantic Council should be urged to obtain from the Ministerial Meeting of the Council at the time of the Annual Review a paper setting out the reactions of the Ministerial Meeting to resolutions put forward by this Conference."[6]

Unfortunately, little has happened since that resolution was approved in 1959 to suggest either that the military recommendations have been given serious consideration or that in any event major progress was being made toward overcoming the problems the Committee had singled out.

Political Committee

The Political Committee has produced in eleven sessions some 54 resolutions, nearly three-fourths of them declarative in nature. The latter type have included resolutions on disarmament, Berlin, European integration, Eastern Europe, underdeveloped countries, European security, China's attack on India, and the Cuban crisis. All but a handful of these were dealt with in two or more successive annual sessions. Most of the declarative resolutions were prompted by specific events. All were in essence broad restatements of basic Western policy, although in the case of disarmament the Conference, in its last two pronouncements, went beyond that policy by endorsing the idea of an eventual International Police Force, regretting the failure of "the governments concerned" to make progress in this sphere and recommending "the

---

[6]U. S. Senate, Fifth NATO Parliamentarians' Conference (November 16-20, 1959), 8th Congress, 2d Session, February 11, 1960, p. 9-10.

appointment of experts to examine the technical aspects of control and inspection and general disarmament."[7] The resolutions on European integration, to take another issue illustratively, welcomed the progress of the Six but warned of the "danger of economic divisions" between them and the remainder of the OEEC and declared further that "European integration should not encourage the delusion that Europe, no [sic] more than North America, can stand alone...."[8] In similar vein, the Political Committee took due note of the shifting relationships both within the Alliance and between East and West and declared that "... The phase in which the United States has generously accepted most of the burdens and responsibilities of the Alliance has to progress towards a phase in which those burdens and responsibilities will be more equitably shared." The Conference accordingly expressed the "wish" for a "re-appraisal of the organization, the objectives and means of action of NATO"[9] and in the following year it urged prompt ratification of the agreement establishing the OECD.[10]

Most of the Political Committee's few strictly operative resolutions dealt with three nongovernmental organizations, recommending the establishment of the Atlantic Congress, the Atlantic Convention of NATO Nations and the Atlantic Institute. All three groups subsequently came into existence. The NPC's sponsorship, dating from the Third Session (1957), may well have had an important part in the outcome — the more so since the first two organizations required legislative action and the third depends in part on governmental subsidies. The Atlantic Congress was a brilliant international celebration of the tenth anniversary of the Alliance. In prestige if not in catalytic political effect it lived up to its advance billing as "comparable to the Hague Congress of 1948,"[11] which helped launch the European unity movement, and it gave further impetus to the proposed establishment of a permanent

---

[7]NPC, Reports and Resolutions, 6th Session, November 21-26, 1960, p. 43; Ibid., 5th Session, November 16-20, 1959, Senate Report, p. 6.

[8]U. S. Senate, Fifth NATO Parliamentarians' Conference, op. cit., p. 3-4.

[9]Ibid., p. 6-7.

[10]NPC, op. cit., p. 42.

[11]NPC, op. cit., 3d Session, November 11-16, 1957, p. 7.

Atlantic Institute. The Atlantic Convention of NATO Nations, which met in Paris January 8 to 20, 1962, was an officially appointed conference of "leading representative citizens" with a mandate to "convene as often as necessary in order to examine exhaustively and to recommend how greater coopera- tion and unity of purpose...within the Atlantic Community may best be developed."[12] Although its work was hardly ex- haustive, the Convention produced specific recommendations, embodied in the "Declaration of Paris," at least one of which has engaged the active and prompt attention of some govern- ment officials and parliamentary leaders,[13] and all of which will provide for some time to come a basis of thought and discussion and agitation for those interested in strengthening the institutional arrangements of the Atlantic Community.

The NPC and its Political Committee have been less suc- cessful in their repeated efforts to encourage more effective consultation within the North Atlantic Council. In 1956, the Conference recalled the commitment of the Treaty partners, under Article 4, to "consult together whenever, in the opinion of any of them, the territorial integrity, political independence or security of any of the Parties is threatened." The NPC resolution stressed "the need for (a) full and reasonable scope to be given by the North Atlantic Council to the interpretation of this Article; (b) the consultation to be political as well as military; (c) the consultation to be as far as possible between Ministers ..." and "calls upon" the Council to proceed ac- cordingly.[14] The next year, after Suez and Hungary had pointed up the hazards of non-consultation, the Conference began a similar resolution with the observation that "the governments do not seem to have given consideration to the Political Reso- lution voted last year ..." and concluded it by "requesting governments to consult together insofar as practicable before a decision is taken by any one of them which may affect Western solidarity.[15]

---

[12]Ibid.

[13]Viz., "To Develop the NATO Parliamentarians' Conference into a consultative assembly which would review the work of all Atlantic insti- tutions and make recommendations to them." "Declaration of Paris," op. cit.

[14]Text of this 2d Annual Conference resolution in NPC, op. cit., 3d Session, 1957, Appendix B, p. 71.

[15]Ibid., p. 8.

The Fourth Conference, held in 1958, noting that the Secretary General had "reported encouraging developments in consultations on political matters within the Atlantic Council," expressed "satisfaction with the degree of implementation given to former resolutions of the Council and of the NATO Parliamentarians' Conference on consultation. . . ." The resolution went on, however, to regret "that this consultation has not always resulted in the expected cooperation." It ended by stressing the need for the Council to "continue to develop its consultation techniques" and suggested that the new methods and the results and the needs for further improvements be made "the subject of another high level review, study and report."[16] In the Fifth Session, in 1958, the Conference recommended that the Heads of Goverment meet annually. It also noted some further progress: "Regular and intimate consultations between all NATO members have increased the sense of mutual solidarity and are therefore to be welcomed, as is to be welcomed the fact that in preparation for the East-West Summit Meeting two sessions of the NATO Council are to be held on December 15th and December 22nd."[17]

The Conference was silent on the problem at its sixth and seventh sessions and reverted to it only briefly at the eighth session, in 1962, when it recommended that the governments set themselves the objective, inter alia, "To harmonise political, military and economic policy on matters affecting the Atlantic Community as a whole."[18] At the fifth session, Secretary General Spaak had reported some progress and some backsliding in the matter of consultation, and had called attention to the inevitable difficulties of this diplomatie á quinze; finally, he had suggested that it was several years too early to know whether the practice would prove a success or a failure.[19] As another NATO official has remarked, progress in this area "is not conspicuous to the public, and it is not always easy, even for those who are directly concerned

---

[16]U. S. Senate, Fourth NATO Parliamentarians' Conference, op. cit. (November 15-21, 1958), 86th Congress, 1st Session, 1959, p. 7.

[17]U. S. Senate, Fifth NATO Parliamentarians' Conference, op. cit., p. 3.

[18]NPC, op. cit., 8th Session, November 12-16, 1962, p. 48.

[19]NPC, Verbatim Report, Fifth Annual Conference, November 19, 1959, p. 118-120. See also George Ball, ibid., 8th Session, November 16, p.m., 1962, p. 53-54.

in the work, to identify results or to see precisely where national policies have been influenced by the exchanges that
have taken place within NATO."[20]

Since the NPC is once-removed from the process, its influence is even more problematical and difficult to evaluate.
Nevertheless, the perfecting of consultation within NATO is a
subject on which it would seem particularly appropriate for
the Conference to exert a continuing influence. It is one of
several subjects on which the Conference might well seek to
obtain regular annual reports from the NATO Secretary General. Specific sins of omission on the part of the member
governments would then become more discernible, and a constructive pressure could be more sharply focused, not only
through Conference resolutions but by means of parliamentary
questions or their equivalent in the national legislatures.
That genuine consultation, as the NPC has noted, does not
always lead to concerted policies is another and more difficult problem. But its solution would be facilitated by a growing
habit of consultation, to which the NPC and its Political Committee should be able to make a significant contribution in
the coming years.

Economic Committee

Perhaps the most important and difficult problem the
Conference encountered in the economic field was to reach
an understanding as to what NATO's competence should be
and how that should affect the NPC's own terms of reference.
Under Article 23 of the Rules of Procedure, the NPC appointed
a committee "for matters arising under Article 2 of the North
Atlantic Treaty." The Economic Committee as such was
established in the Third Session, replacing and growing out
of the Economic Section of the now defunct General Affairs
Committee that had functioned during the Second and Third
Sessions. At the latter session the Conference declared that
"...the implementation [of Article 2] should be a prime objective both of the Governments of NATO countries and of the
NATO Parliamentarians' Conference." The resolution urged
the governments and instructed the Standing Committee "to

---

[20]Sir Evelyn Shuckburgh, Assistant Secretary General for Political
Affairs of NATO, "Political Consultation" (Paris, NATO Information
Service, May 1960), n.p.

keep under review progress made by the North Atlantic Council and by member governments in the implementation of Article 2." [21]

The relevant portion of that article states simply that the parties "will seek to eliminate conflict in their international economic policies and will encourage economic collaboration between any or all of them." Notwithstanding much clamor among advocates of Atlantic unity in favor of implementing those provisions, they have remained largely a dead letter. As Secretary General Spaak acknowledged to the Fifth Session (1959), in this domain "the progress and successes of the Organization are extremely modest." [22]

The reasons were clear enough. Throughout the 1950's at least, the NATO framework was both too broad for economic integration and too narrow for economic cooperation. Inter-governmental economic cooperation among the Alliance partners, including for practical purposes the United States and Canada, was the province of the OEEC, and was soon to become even more clearly that of the OECD. The Alliance had been established for reasons of military security, and there were some who felt that the addition of economic functions would be an undesirable diversion. As for economic integration, only six continental members appeared ready for that. Britain had resisted for nearly a decade urgent proposals to make it a Community of seven, and there was little doubt that the United States and Canada, which had not been invited, would be even more reticent. The scope for a NATO economic function was evidently limited. Indeed, in the Fifth Session, Secretary General Spaak urged that before elaborating too many economic resolutions, the parliamentarians make an effort to decide once and for all whether or not Article 2 had been a mistake and, if not, precisely what competence NATO should acquire in this field. His suggestion was sound for several reasons, including the one he singled out for the NPC: "It is necessary that one no longer be able, when proposals are presented to NATO, to take refuge behind a negative position of principle." [23]

---

[21]NPC, op. cit., 3d Session, November 11–16, 1957, p. 9.

[22]NPC, Verbatim Report, 5th Session, November 19, 1959, p. 109–110.

[23]Ibid., p. 110.

Spaak did not venture to answer the questions he had raised. As late as 1959 the conference had envisaged, as an alternative to "an Organization for Atlantic Economic Cooperation," the creation of "a NATO Economic Council."[24] The establishment of the OECD on October 1, 1961, did not of course put an end to agitation for an Atlantic executive, but so far as the NPC was concerned, it seemed to obviate the case for a NATO economic agency.

In its Sixth Session (1960), the Conference welcomed the achievement of "an agreement on establishing OECD" and declared that "a number of the principal objectives incorporated in the resolutions adopted by the Conference require the establishment" of such a body. It recommended "that all parliaments concerned will ratify the agreement without delay...."[25] Its resolutions in subsequent sessions referred frequently to the need for coordination of various policies among the Alliance partners but did not revert to the notion of new economic institutions for NATO. For the governments and the parliamentarians of Atlantica, the OECD had become the chosen instrument of economic collaboration.

In an important sense, this development helped clarify the terms of reference of the NPC. After five years of uncertainty, an Atlantic parliamentary organ found itself confronted with an Atlantic intergovernmental agency in the economic domain. From the organizational point of view, there remained one serious anomaly: four nations of Europe — Sweden, Switzerland, Austria and Ireland — were full members of the latter but determined non-members of the former.

It is in part for this reason that the NATO Parliamentarians and some of their governments have begun to study the possibilities of reorganizing the NPC. This indeed was foreshadowed in a further recommendation of the 6th Conference suggesting that "authorized members of all the parliaments of countries of the OECD should meet from time to time to consider matters of common interest arising under the working of OECD."[26]

---

[24]U. S. Senate, Fifth NATO Parliamentarians' Conference, op. cit., p. 7.

[25]NPC, op. cit., 6th Session, November 21–26, 1960, p. 57.

[26]Ibid.

In the Seventh Session (1961), Secretary General Dirk U. Stikker offered some pertinent comments on the economic potential of NATO:

> ... There are certain limitations on what NATO can achieve in the economic field. It is not an executive agency for economic policy. It has no power to implement decisions. There are other international bodies operating in this sphere on whose attributions it cannot infringe. Nevertheless, the influence which NATO can exert in economic matters, both collectively and through its constituent members, is by no means negligible; and it seems to me that it has increased of recent years both because the economic threat of the Soviet bloc (a problem which can be adequately dealt with in no other international body) has become even more clearly apparent, and because the necessity for an increased defence effort, with all its economic implications, has become so evident.[27]

The appropriate NATO function in economic affairs, Stikker suggested, was illustrated by the Council's effort to reapportion the defense burden in the light of specific difficulties — at that moment those presented by Britain's balance of payments. It was illustrated in another way by NATO's appointment of an international mission to "examine the problems involved in a balanced economic development of Greece and Turkey."[28] It remained for Senator Jacob K. Javits, who had served as Chairman of the NPC's Economic Committee since its inception, to describe the evolution of this issue within the Economic Committee and offer a definition that appears to have received the agreement of the Conference:

> To my mind, the meeting of the Economic Committee this time demonstrated the validity of a concept which is historic and which we are now about to engage in: that is, a clear delineation of what part of the economic affairs of the Atlantic Community is inherent in the NATO Alliance.... What economic function is left in NATO, and what economic function will pass to OECD, is now — it seems to me — undergoing a clarifying

[27]NPC, Addresses by Speakers, 7th Session, November 13-17, 1961, p. 20.

[28]Ibid.

treatment, and the Resolutions which have been brought
in by the Economic Committee begin to make that
crystal clear.[29]

Senator Javits listed four economic questions with which NATO
should deal: economic warfare, aid to the underdeveloped
partners of NATO, the economic capabilities of member
states for defense, and trade with the Communist bloc. He
noted that the OECD could more appropriately deal with trade
generally and with aid to the less-developed countries and
declared that the emergence of that agency would serve to
take Article 2 of the NATO Treaty "out of the fuzzy stage."
In consequence, he concluded, "there is a great opportunity
for NATO to be far more effective in the economic field than
ever before."[30]

The resolutions presented by the Economic Committee at
that Session and adopted by the Conference were, it must be
said, of broader scope than that defined by the Committee
Chairman. Indeed the 46 resolutions originated by the Economic Committee to date embrace the widest conceivable
range of economic questions, and there is no discernible
trend toward narrowing the scope. Of that total, nearly 75
percent have been of the declarative variety, recommending
in effect the "earnest efforts" of NATO governments to
"harmonize" or "coordinate" specified policies in largely
unspecified ways. In such terms the Committee and the Conference have pronounced on East-West trade, commodity
price stabilization, aid to developing countries, multilateral
investment guarantees, balance of payments problems, international dumping, early manufactures markets, non-tariff
trade barriers, the European Economic Community and most
of the UN-affiliated economic agencies.

In the Seventh Session, Senator Javits reported that his Committee had reformulated the definition of the NPC's economic
competence so as to embrace four areas: economic warfare,
the "economic consequences of military preparedness,"

---

[29]NPC, Verbatim Report, November 25, p.m., 1960, p. 50.

[30]Ibid., p. 51. This delimitation was essentially similar to that recommended by NATO's Committee of Three and adopted by the Council
on December 13, 1956. See Report of the Committee of Three on non-
Military Cooperation in NATO (Paris: NATO Information Division,
December 14, 1956), Part II, paras. 62, 63, 64 and 65; and Part III,
para. 66.

problems of the less-developed NATO allies, and "the formulation of a caucus view of the NATO Parliamentarians for
presentation in the OECD."[31] The last-mentioned category
is of course the key to almost unlimited competence in international economics. The proposed "formulation of a caucus
view," it should be noted, was conceived as a function of the
NATO Parliamentarians, not the NATO Council. Senator
Javits had in fact indicated previously his view that resent-
ment of other OECD members would be understandable if the
NATO governments were to concert their OECD policies outside of OECD.[32] The "caucus" was to remain essentially a
parliamentary function and — unless or until the OECD ac-
quired a consultative assembly of its own — it was clearly a
function that would leave the NATO Parliamentarians a far
wider scope than that of the NATO Council. It was a function
also that inevitably would commit the Conference to a juris-
dictional rivalry with the Consultative Assembly of the Council
of Europe. It had become clear in any event that the Conference was unlikely to be further troubled by the uncertainties expressed earlier as to which "economic affairs" of
NATO members are "susceptible of consideration by NATO
for coordination within the NATO framework" or what contribution can be made "within the NATO framework" to the
work of other agencies.[33]

If the Economic Committee has been general and far-
ranging in its approach to resolutions, it has also furnished
one of the most impressive examples to date of what can
happen when an international parliamentary assembly addresses itself to a timely subject, makes concrete and fully-
considered recommendations, and then follows up to assure
their implementation.

In the Eighth Session (1962), the Conference adopted a recommendation initiated by Senator Javits which found it necessary and appropriate "that all nations of the Atlantic Community should join in the task now being undertaken through the Alliance for Progress," without diminishing similar efforts

---

[31]NPC, Verbatim Report, 7th Session, November 17, p.m., 1961, p.
46.

[32]Ibid., 6th Session, November 25, p.m., 1960, p. 51. This possibility
had been noted earlier by the NATO Committee of Three.

[33]Ibid., Resolutions and Reports, 3d Session, November 12-16, 1957,
p. 13.

elsewhere, and accordingly proposed an international conference to consider measures "to enlist the private and public
sectors of the member nations of the OECD."[34] A working
party was appointed to help organize the project.

What made the proposal important and unusual was first
that it put before two trans-Atlantic bodies the problem of
Latin American development, and secondly, that the initial
steps in its implementation were not to be left to chance or
the executive agencies. Senator Javits personally sought the
support of key leaders in Europe and Latin America as well
as the United States. On April 23, 1963, he was able to an-
nounce the establishment of the Atlantic Community Development Group for Latin America (ADELA) with the purpose of
"pulling together over the next 6 to 12 months immediate-
impact, private-investment projects on a tripartite basis."[35]
This group, headed by a tripartite directorate of economists,[36]
with a Secretary drawn from the Senator's Washington staff,
was financed by the Ford Foundation and by U. S., European
and Latin American foundations and business firms. Bipartisan support in the United States was strengthened by the
participation of then Senator Hubert H. Humphrey. After ex-
ploring matters with many interests and organizations, including top officials of the OECD, the Inter-American Development Bank and the Organization of American States, and
after convening the proposed conference, in January 1964,
ADELA's Directors took steps that led, on September 24, 1964,
to the incorporation of the ADELA Investment Company. By
early 1966, the company comprised 130 participating business
and financial firms in Europe, the United States, Canada and
Japan. It had invested $16.8 million in 26 enterprises in 13
Latin American countries and was holding the balance of its

---

[34]NPC, ibid., 8th Session, November 12-16, 1962, p. 61-62.

[35]Sen. Javits in Congressional Record, 88th Congress, 1st Session,
April 23, 1963 (offprint).

[36]Viz., Julio Gonzalez del Solar, European Representative of the
Inter-American Development Bank; Dr. Aurelio Peccei, Managing Director, Italconsult; Warren Wilhelm, Foreign Manager of the Economics Department, Texaco, Inc. The Secretary was Herbert J. Blitz of
Washington.

capital, $16.9 million, in non-operational investments in seven Latin American countries.[37]

The success of this undertaking is attributable in great part to the prodigious amount of preparation and follow-up by the Committee under Senator Javits' leadership. In addition to the meetings, correspondence and reports that preceded and followed the Eighth Session, this particular effort benefited from the adoption of a device new to the NPC, namely that of "country advisory groups," organized so far in the United States and Germany, to assist and advise the Committee members in their own country.

The evolution of this project illustrates and bolsters the case for concentrating the efforts of the NPC on specific proposals adequately prepared. It also points up the need to strengthen the staff services available to the NPC and its committees. Senator Javits, in summing up the work of his committee, told the Eighth Conference:

> Everyone is literally breaking their backs to do what ought to be done by an effective Secretariat with much more purpose and centralisation of authority.... It will be noted... that practically every staff paper was drawn up by the Rapporteur, the Vice-Chairman or the Chairman.... This is not just a matter of work, it is also a matter of responsibility which should be centralised in an effective Secretariat where it properly belongs.[38]

Members of the Scientific and Technical Committee have reached a similar conclusion.

Scientific and Technical Committee

No committee of the NPC and few from other consultative assemblies can claim a more satisfactory record of implementation than that of the Scientific and Technical Committee.

[37]ADELA, press release, January 5, 1966, and "General Information" brochure (n.d.). See also memorandum of September 16, 1963, and "Report of the Executive Directors," April 1964. The ADELA Investment Company, S.A., of which Dr. Marcus Wallenberg of Sweden is Chairman, has its head office at 13 Blvd. de la Foire, Luxembourg and an operations office in Lima, Peru.

[38]NPC, Verbatim Report, 8th Session, November 16, 1962, a.m., p. 30.

The establishment of such a committee had not been contemplated at the outset. In the Second Session (1956) the Economic Committee and plenary adopted a proposal of Senator
Henry M. Jackson to set up a Special Committee on Scientific
and Technical Personnel, with instructions to report to the
Third Conference on measures needed to improve and augment
the training and utilization of such personnel within the NATO
area. That report recommended, among other things, that the
committee be made a permanent body of the Conference, and
in the Fourth Session the Scientific and Technical Committee,
under the Chairmanship of Senator Jackson, took its place
with the other four. By 1960, the Committee was able to make
the following report of results to the Sixth Conference:

> Initiatives taken by this Conference, upon the recom-
> mendation of its Scientific and Technical Committee,
> have been directly responsible for NATO-wide efforts
> to reinforce and supplement national scientific pro-
> grammes.
>
> Specifically, this Conference took the lead in estab-
> lishing the NATO Science Fellowship Programme, the
> NATO Advanced Study Institute Programme, and a NATO
> Research Programme.
>
> The NATO Science Advisor and the NATO Science
> Advisory Committee are now assisting the NATO
> Council in developing community-wide programs for
> the improvement of science.
>
> In short, the NATO Science Programme is now a
> going concern. It works; it is producing results; it is
> engaged in imaginative forward planning across a
> broad front.[39]

Back of those results lay a series of specific, detailed and
comprehensive proposals, well-timed and relatively modest.
These were embodied in a 7000-word report prepared and
submitted by Senator Jackson to the Third Conference. The
report noted that NATO was confronted with "a genuine crisis
in the form of serious shortages of skilled scientific and
technical manpower," due chiefly to the scientific revolution,
and that the Soviet Union was turning out trained scientific
manpower at twice the per capita rate of the Atlantic

---

[39]NPC, op. cit., 6th Session, November 21-26, 1960, p. 19-20.

Community. NATO should become a catalyst of national and trans-Atlantic efforts to remove all "barriers to the development of talent." To that end the Committee recommended the following: a NATO-sponsored and financed "Talent Development Programme, designed to produce annually at least 500 doctoral degree holders," at an estimated cost of $8 to $10 million a year; a NATO awards program in mathematics or science for secondary school students and teachers, at an estimated annual cost of $1,600,000; an increase in the number and variety of summer study institutes through NATO contributions, estimated at an initial $100,000 a year, to existing programs; cooperative research in meteorology and other subjects under NATO contracts; the immediate establishment of a NATO Defense Missile Training Center in anticipation of integrating defensive missiles into the NATO armed forces; the immediate establishment of a North Atlantic Institute for Defense Studies (AIDS) to serve SHAPE somewhat as the Rand Corporation serves the U. S. Air Force. The report as approved (but not the resolution) also recommended increased exchange programs in this field and agreements on the equivalence of diplomas; "a European-wide scientific and engineering employment clearing house"; an information program to focus public attention on the manpower problem, including an annual "stock-taking report" under NPC sponsorship; establishment of an Atlantic Community Foundation working under a NATO contract as the coordinator of the scientific manpower activities sponsored by the Alliance.[40]

Subsequent resolutions adopted in the Fourth and Fifth Sessions noted with satisfaction that the OEEC was making its first survey of national policies in this field and initiating programs for the exchange of scientific and technical knowledge; recommended measures aimed at improving the study of Asian and African languages; suggested "the early appointment of a NATO Language-Area Advisor" and emphasized the desirability of increasing the Science Fellowship program and of developing NATO research programs.[41] In the Sixth Session, the Conference welcomed the report of Louis Armand's NATO Study Group on "Increasing the Effectiveness of Western Science," regretted the failure to implement the

---

[40]NPC, 3d Session, November 11-16, 1957, p. 31-48 and p. 19.

[41]NPC, op. cit., 4th Session, November 15-21, 1958 (Senate Report), p. 9-11; and ibid., 5th Session, November 16-20, 1959 (Senate Report), p. 10-11.

language-study proposal; and urged rapid completion of a NATO study on establishment of an International Institute of Science and Technology.[42] By the Eighth Session, the NATO Scientific Committee's final report on such an institute had been published, and the Conference supported its establishment. That project, which had been suggested in the Armand report of 1960 with a view to providing Western Europe with an institution comparable to the Massachusetts Institute of Technology, has received heavy emphasis in NPC reports since the Sixth Session.[43]

In the first eleven sessions of the NPC, the Scientific and Technical Committee adopted 36 resolutions. Of these, 18 could be classified as operative — by far the highest ratio among the committees. The Committee's comparative success in obtaining the implementation of its recommendations is attributable in part to the fact that most of its objectives have been comparatively modest and hence more readily attainable than, for example, recommendations of the Military Committee on NATO force levels and equipment standardization. Clearly, however, the Committee's achievements are also attributable in part to the concreteness and relevance of many of its resolutions and to the thoroughness of the study and investigation that preceded their drafting.

Cultural Affairs and Information Committee

Under Article 2 of the North Atlantic Treaty, the parties undertook to strengthen their "free institutions" and to bring about "a better understanding of the principles upon which these institutions are founded...." As with the economic provisions of that article, the implementation of the information clause has, in the view of the NPC and most other friendly critics of NATO, left much to be desired. The activities of NATO itself have been largely confined to sponsoring tours and briefings for journalists and others, the publication of a monthly newsletter and the NATO Handbook, and the preparation of a small number of films for use by educational groups and the Allied armed forces. Within the Organization this

---

[42]NPC, op. cit., 6th Session, November 21–26, 1960, p. 61–63.

[43]The Killian Report has estimated the institute would cost $56 million to establish and $16 million a year to run.

work is carried out by the Information Division of the Secretariat under the guidance of a Committee on Information and Cultural Relations. Conferences of information officials from member governments have been held on two occasions in what were largely vain efforts to strengthen the programs. Official activities in this field have been supplemented in varying degrees by the efforts of private organizations, notably the Atlantic Treaty Association and its national affiliates.

There is no doubt that public understanding of the Alliance is deficient. As the Secretary General noted in 1954, a survey the previous year by the International Press Institute revealed that 79 percent of the people of the United States, 82 percent of the British, 87 percent of the Italians and 89 percent of the French "had no idea of what NATO or OTAN stood for."[44] As an institution, NATO even today probably is less well known to the publics of its member countries and enjoys less prestige, than the United Nations. In the context of the world "struggle for the minds of men," Western observers are often haunted by the paradox that while the West has a far more appealing case, it has never found the means of putting it across and that both at home and abroad the Western countries are kept constantly on the defensive by Communist propaganda.

As one group of authorities put it recently, "The democratic West has not presented forcefully enough either to non-Westerners or even to influential intellectual milieus within its own ranks the social failures of communism and the immense improvement throughout the last century of the average citizen's lot in the North Atlantic area."[45] This concern has led to elaborate attempts to edit a Western "Manifesto" and to innumerable proposals for intensifying the information activies of Western governments and their international agencies.[46]

---

[44]Lord Ismay, NATO: The First Five Years, op. cit., p. 154.

[45]Robert Strausz-Hupé, et al., op. cit., p. 275.

[46]The proposed manifesto was an early project of the Atlantic Institute. The Atlantic Congress Report (London: 1959, p. 56 and 57) is of particular interest in this regard, representing the agreed views of some 600 Western leaders as to what NATO and the member governments should do in this field.

The Cultural Affairs and Information Committee of the NPC, which emerged in the Fourth Session as an outgrowth of the former General Affairs Committee, has proved on the whole less active than the other committees. One reason is that much of what might have been its cultural affairs function has been preempted by the Scientific and Technical Committee. Another reason is that the Committee remains in doubt as to "what action properly belongs to NATO" in this field.[47] The Conference has sponsored information resolutions at every session since the Second, but the Committee has issued only four reports.[48]

The work of the NPC in this field would benefit from more adequate information as to existing programs, as it recognized when in 1962 it urged the North Atlantic Council to "initiate a review procedure to survey annually the foreign and domestic information policies and efforts of member governments."[49]

One of the Committee's main preoccupations, and the subject of its first report, was the establishment of the Atlantic Institute. While the recollection of the Committee and the NPC was faulty in claiming in 1961 that "the idea of an Atlantic Institute originated with the Conference,"[50] there is little doubt that its collective support for the proposal and the labors of some of its members outside the Conference had a good deal to do with the successful launching of that enterprise.

The remainder of the resolutions of this Committee have been devoted largely to noting the inadequacy of NATO information activities, proposing conferences or studies looking toward a clarification of the possibilities and endorsing an intensification of effort generally.

In 1956 the Conference recommended that the NATO Secretary General

---

[47]NPC, op. cit., 8th Session, November 12-16, 1962, p. 72.

[48]Ibid., 6th Session, November 21-26, 1960, p. 25-35; 9th Session, November 4-9, 1963 (F. 185--Rev. 1), n.p.

[49]Ibid., 8th Session, November 12-16, 1962, p. 72.

[50]Ibid., 7th Session, November 13-17, 1961, p. 57. See also ibid., 3d Session, p. 15; 5th Session, p. 12; and 6th Session, p. 67.

produce a publication which would constitute a picture
and complete documentation of the achievements, the
power and the possibilities of NATO, and of the Atlantic
Community, and their physical, demographic, military,
economic, moral, social, scientific and intellectual re-
serves, and those of the nations which belong geographically or spiritually to the Atlantic world and are
or will be certainly at NATO's side to arrest and finally
overcome the Soviet will to impose its domination over
the whole world. [51]

Two years later the Committee took note of the not surprising
fact that there had been "no apparent attempt to begin to implement this recommendation" and invited the NATO Secretary General to look into it. The proposal was quietly dropped
after the Committee was informed by one of its members the
following year that in the opinion of the Secretary General
"it would be extremely difficult for the NATO Secretariat to
undertake a work which went beyond the geographical borders
of the NATO Alliance and which did not limit itself to actual
resources, but also discussed potentials." [52]

In 1958 the Committee recommended that its officers report the following year on ways to "assimilate and dissemi-
nate information" on the "aims, functions and achievements of
NATO." It further invited the Secretary General to "convene
a conference of persons particularly well qualified to undertake a complete and comparative study of the teaching pro-
grammes and educational systems in the member countries." [53]
The next year it contented itself largely with endorsing the
information resolutions of the Atlantic Congress which had
suggested inter alia that NATO "raise the status" of the office
of the Director of Information, give it a larger budget and
"greater freedom to develop imaginative basic information
materials" and provide it with a fund to encourage and assist
the work of appropriate voluntary organizations.[54]   The

---

[51]NPC, op. cit., 3d Session, November 11-16, 1957, p. 16.

[52]NPC, Summary of Meeting of the Cultural Affairs and Information
Committee, October 4, 1961, p. 1 (Doc. D.102).

[53]U. S. Senate, Fourth NATO Parliamentarians' Conference, op. cit.,
p. 9.

[54]U. S. Senate, Fifth NATO Parliamentarians' Conference, op. cit.,
p. 11-12.

Conference reverted to these proposals in 1961 with a view to "the assumption of the initiative by the free world in the war of ideas." It further called for "the use of the external broadcasting facilities of the member nations ... as an international radio network" and urged the NATO Council "to study the use of television as a further means of conveying information to the peoples of the Soviet Union and their satellites." [55]

In the Eighth Session (1962) the Conference requested the North Atlantic Council "to convene a conference of representatives of appropriate authorities ... to recommend the best means of ... creating interest in and support for the Atlantic idea, especially among young people." It further recommended that the action of member governments be "intensified and coordinated"; that the Council "investigate ways of improving the dissemination of objective information by the West"; that, as noted above, it "decide what action properly belongs to NATO" and institute an annual review of pertinent activity; and that "increased money and staff be made available to NATO by governments to carry out tasks in this field." [56]

The Cultural Affairs and Information Committee has produced four reports and 24 recommendations since 1956. Apart perhaps from the special publication it recommended in 1957, its resolutions might be characterized as unexceptionable if also uninspired. There is no doubt that a larger NATO information budget would make possible a greater variety and quantity of pertinent material for use by governmental and voluntary agencies and would permit the regular reporting and analysis of existing activities out of which the best ideas

---

[55]NPC, op. cit., 7th Session, November 13-17, 1961, p. 57. Lord Ismay (op. cit., p. 155) notes that NATO "as an organisation, has never envisaged carrying on propaganda" to the Soviet bloc, but that as between the views that psychological warfare was appropriately a NATO or was purely a national function, "a compromise has been reached whereby NATO can act as a forum for consultation" in this field.

[56]NPC, op. cit., 8th Session, November 12-16, 1962, p. 71-72. See also Senator Karl E. Mundt's speech in NPC, Verbatim Report, 8th Session, November 16, a.m., 1962, p. 41-42. The annual information budget was there reported as 2.800.000 N.F. or considerably less than $600,000. In 1963 the Committee issued its second report and recommended inter alia that NATO's information budget be increased by 50 percent.

and procedures might be further developed and more widely applied.

As in other fields, however, there are limits to what NATO as such can and should do, because it is essentially the agency of a military alliance. The most important image for NATO as such to project is that of a strong, dynamic and determined force ready to defend its members against aggression. The establishment of that image depends far more on facts unproclaimed than on aims and principles declared and reiterated. Moreover, the great values and human achievements that the Alliance was created to defend are enjoyed and cherished by a far larger number of countries than those that today contribute to its defense effort. The informational function of NATO remains hampered by the fact that the organization is narrow both functionally and geographically. Its essentially military character imposes the additional problem of security. Lord Ismay has written, "Time and again the release of an interesting story has had to be forbidden because it deals with a subject which is classified."

Under existing arrangements, furthermore, as the first Secretary General has pointed out, the Organization's activities "are limited to initiation, suggestion and coordination: the responsibility for implementation rests with the governments who, naturally, are free to adopt, reject or adapt the suggestions as they think fit. Governments, of course, have their own difficulties about NATO information: not all are equally well staffed or equipped to distribute this information; ... again, in some countries state information agencies can work only in restricted fields as laid down by law." Lord Ismay noted, however, that some member governments are endeavoring to overcome some of the obstacles by assigning an official to deal specifically with NATO information matters and that the Council's information committee is "gradually developing a 'NATO way' of handling and solving information problems."[57]

The improvement of NATO information is obviously in the first instance a problem for the member governments. As John McGowan, then NATO Information Director, told the Committee in 1961, according to the summary report, "NATO's information specialists are primarily technicians and advisers, not makers of information policy or direct 'retailers'

---

[57]Op. cit., p. 154-155.

of material." Some governments were doing more than others, although "with respect to NATO's requests for cooperation on specific projects, responses have always been good." Attempts to improve the NATO output by the inclusion of "controversial" material had met with only partial success because "distinct limits were posed by the nervousness (often understandable) of some of the member countries."[58] The experience of the Cultural Affairs and Information Committee suggests, in short, that the NPC might enhance its record in this area, as in others, by focusing on limited, concrete objectives and exerting pressure at the national level.

THE PROBLEM OF OFFICIAL STATUS

In its Eleventh Session (1965), the NATO Parliamentarians' Conference unanimously agreed to look into the prospects of acquiring official status as a means of strengthening its influence in Atlantic affairs. On a motion by Sir Geoffrey de Freitas, one of the founders of the NPC, the Conference instructed its Political Committee to prepare a report on the possibility of converting the organization into "a Consultative Assembly of NATO, in an official relationship to the North Atlantic Council." The resolution urged all NATO parliaments "to consider the conditions of a possible improvement of the status and the efficiency of the NATO Parliamentarians' Conference." It also noted with regret "the lack of progress in creating an Atlantic Consultative Assembly."[59] The vote expressed a sense of concern and frustration that has been increasingly evident within the Conference since its Second Session. The decision came at an inauspicious time in the affairs of the Alliance, but the Conference will have little to lose and ultimately much to gain from a comprehensive examination of the matter.

---

[58]NPC, Summary of Meeting of the Cultural Affairs and Information Committee, op. cit., p. 2.

[59]U.S. Senate, Eleventh NATO Parliamentarians' Conference (October 4-9, 1965), 89th Congress, 1st Session, December 15, 1965, p. 40-41. For discussion of the NPC's effort in 1962 and 1963 to establish a consultative Atlantic Assembly, see above, p. 9-12 and below, p. 129-136.

One of the first advocates of such a study was Paul-Henri
Spaak. The Belgian statesman, then Secretary General of
NATO, told the Fifth Session of the NPC in 1959:

> I am more and more persuaded — I have always been,
> but now more than ever — that an organisation like the
> Atlantic Organisation cannot prosper and develop with-
> out the real support of a parliamentary elite. I would
> add that, often, I have the impression that a genuine
> parliamentary supervision would not be a useless thing
> in the Atlantic Organisation. For the moment I am,
> personally, more a civil servant than a politician....
> Well, the experience I am now acquiring only confirms
> my political experience, and I believe I can say that
> for an administrative service, the fear of a parliament
> is the beginning of wisdom.[60]

Spaak went on to caution that the difficulties of establishing
parliamentary supervision over the Atlantic Community would
be "enormous," partly because there was no common idea
within the area as to what such a body's role, competence,
powers or place in public life ought to be. Europe had learned
from experience how dangerous it was to create political and
parliamentary assemblies without power; the Consultative
Assembly of the Council of Europe had declined because the
executive authority had never consulted it. Official status for
an assembly offered both advantages and disadvantages that
were difficult to evaluate and that did not necessarily assure
its success. He advised the parliamentarians, who were
better qualified than anyone else, to study the problem and
"to present one day concrete proposals that the governments
will be obliged to examine." It would be, he warned, "an extremely complex and difficult problem to resolve."

Spaak and his successors have given strong assurances of
the interest with which NATO already receives the resolutions
of the Conference. Spaak reported that he and his staff, after
studying them, submitted them to the Permanent Council,
"generally with comments."[61] Stikker told the Conference,
"I have given instructions to my staff to follow most carefully

---

[60]NPC, Verbatim Report, op. cit., 5th Session, November 19, a.m.,
1959, p. 108.

[61]Ibid., p. 106-107.

your debates and to prepare a thorough analysis of them so that it will become another guideline for our action during the twelve months to come."[62] Both officials have pointed out, however, that under present arrangements, neither the Organization nor the member governments had any obligation to act on the recommendations. For Stikker, the conclusion was necessarily and simply that "It is...within the realm of national government that you will have to exercise your direct influence. To say that is not to detract from your importance as a body but to clarify where the real leverage of power is located." He expressed doubt whether NATO could be any more responsive "if you were officially called a NATO Parliamentary Assembly.... On the contrary, I believe that your strength lies in the very fact that your institution has grown up spontaneously and unofficially. In custom, if not in law, you have become an essential institution of NATO. Your legal status seems to me only a very secondary issue."[63]

That view is not without eminent support in the NPC. In the same (Seventh) session the then President, Lord Crathorne, stated, "I am glad that he [Stikker] approved our present informal arrangements, and believe that our strength does, in fact, derive from the informality. After all...the crux of the whole matter...is that NATO is not, and was not intended to be a supranational institution.... Where such power is lacking surely it is better for members to get together informally, as we do, and express our views one with the other." While Lord Crathorne saw "Almost limitless scope" for the Atlantic Community to "evolve gradually and naturally," he advised the Conference to defer the question of "a formal Atlantic parliamentary assembly" until further progress had been made in the creation of a European common market— that is, it could be inferred, one that embraced Britain and other EFTA nations.[64]

This, however, would appear to overlook some of the pertinent evidence. As Spaak had advised the Conference two

---

[62]Ibid., 7th Session, November 13, 1961, p. 12-13.

[63]Ibid. Manlio Brosio, Stikker's successor, has taken a similar position. --NPC, Plenary Verbatim, 10th Session, November 16, a.m., 1964, p. 12.

[64]Ibid., 7th Session, November 16, a.m., 1961, p. 14.

years earlier, the efforts of the Conference to obtain NATO action through requests or recommendations to the Council or the Secretary General actually were inappropriate. They amounted to an attempt "to obtain recognition indirectly of the official character of your organization." Spaak feared that the NATO organs would be unable to act on such Conference resolutions, on the ground that they would thereby appear "to consider as definitively settled, questions that continue to arise."[65] The Conference did not adopt Spaak's suggestion for a thorough study of the entire question until three years later, and it has yet to carry out such a study.

The Conference nevertheless appears to have recognized as early as its Second Session the connection between official status and more effective operation.[66] Shortly before that, the Standing Committee had met with NATO's Committee of Three[67] to urge "the more formal recognition of the Conference...as being of vital importance."[68] The subsequent report of the Three Wise Men, which was approved by the North Atlantic Council on December 13, 1956, became the basis for the present quasi-official status of the NATO Parliamentarians' Conference. The report said:

> Among the best supporters of NATO and its purposes are those Members of Parliament who have had a chance at first hand to see some of its activities and to learn of its problems, and to exchange views with their colleagues from other parliaments. In particular, formation of national Parliamentary Associations and

---

[65]Ibid., 5th Session, November 19, p.m., 1959, p. 107.

[66]NPC, 2d Session, Report of the U. S. House Delegation, 85th Congress, 1st Session, House Report No. 26, February 4, 1957, p. 3. The U. S. delegation commented in that report that "the most exhaustive study and deliberation" should be undertaken "before trying to enlarge the status" of the Conference.--Ibid.

[67]The "Three Wise Men" — the Foreign Ministers of Italy (Gaetano Martino), Norway (Halvard Lange) and Canada (Lester Pearson) — had been named by the Council in May 1956 to consider possibilities for improving political and economic cooperation within the Alliance. They met with the NPC Standing Committee on September 12, 1956.

[68]G. de Freitas, op. cit., p. 12.

the activities of the Conference of Members of Parliament from NATO countries have contributed to the development of public support for NATO and solidarity among its members.

In order to maintain a close relationship of Parliamentarians with NATO, the following arrangements are recommended:

(a) that the Secretary General continue to place the facilities of NATO headquarters at the disposal of Parliamentary Conferences and give all possible help with arrangements for their meetings;

(b) that invited representatives of member governments and the Secretary General and other senior NATO civil and military officers attend certain of these meetings. In this way the parliamentarians would be informed on the state of the Alliance and the problems before it, and the value of their discussions would be increased.[69]

At its Third Session (1957) the Conference adopted a resolution of the Political Committee in which it proposed to go well beyond that official conception. It said that the NPC "suggests that greater permanence, continuity and effectiveness could be given

(a) by the establishment of the principle that the Conference meets at the Headquarters of NATO;

(b) by the preparation each year by the NATO Secretariat, after consultation with the Standing Committee, of a report for discussion at the Annual Conference, and by inviting the North Atlantic Council to delegate one of its members to be present each year;

(c) by setting up a link between the Standing Committee and the North Atlantic Council;

(d) by the setting up of such standing committees by the present Standing Committee as are deemed

---

[69] Report of the Committee of Three on Non-Military Cooperation in NATO (Paris: NATO Information Division, December 14, 1956), Section 2 (IV).

appropriate and helpful to the work of the Conference
so far as funds will permit.[70]

In the following session, the Conference was concerned
with the ability of its committees to perform their tasks adequately. A resolution adopted by the Political Committee declared that "these conferences are performing an indispensable
role towards a more efficient working of the North Atlantic
Treaty Organization through debate, information and stimu-
lation on the parliamentary level and with parliamentary
methods." It stressed "the need for appropriate assistance
for Committee work of the Annual NATO Parliamentarians'
Conference in political, military, economic, cultural and
scientific matters."[71]

The NPC's desire for better information and a more
liberal budget was further spelled out at the Fifth Session
(1959):

> With a view to improving the knowledge of, and in-
> creasing the interest in, current NATO questions on
> the Parliamentary level in Member Countries and with
> public opinion at large and enhancing the status of the
> NATO Parliamentary [sic] Conference — the NATO
> Council should ask the Secretary General to prepare a
> comprehensive report each year on the working of the
> alliance during the preceding 12 months, and that this
> report be made available by the Council to the NATO
> Parliamentarians' Conference as aid to their discus-
> sions. The budgetary means of the Annual Conference
> of NATO Parliamentarians should be more adequate to
> the important task of these conferences and they should
> make it possible for interim sessions of the Committees
> to be held at least twice a year.[72]

In the Seventh Session (1961) the Conference once more
called attention to "the many resolutions adopted by the

---

[70] NPC, op. cit., 3d Session, November 11–16, 1957, p. 10.

[71] U. S. Senate, Fourth NATO Parliamentarians' Conference, op. cit.,
p. 7–8.

[72] U. S. Senate, Fifth NATO Parliamentarians' Conference, op. cit.,
p. 5.

Conference in the past," and invited the North Atlantic Council "to submit reports on the action taken on the subjects conceived and the results obtained."[73] By that time, however, it had become clear that such resolutions would remain of little avail so long as the Conference lacked both an adequate budget and a defined, formal relationship with the North Atlantic Council. In the sessions that followed, as will be seen in Chapter 7, the Conference began to focus more purposefully on the problem of correcting those deficiencies.[74]

CONCLUSIONS

If all the claims of its participants were accepted, the NATO Parliamentarians' Conference would be given credit for the establishment of: the Mobile Force;[75] the OECD;[76] the Atlantic Congress;[77] the Atlantic Institute;[78] the Atlantic Convention of NATO Nations;[79] the Atlantic Community Development Group;[80] improved practices of consultation in the North Atlantic Council;[81] the NATO Science Fellowship

---

[73]NPC, op. cit., 6th Session, November 21-26, 1960, p. 42.

[74]See also above, p. 47.

[75]NPC, Verbatim Report, op. cit. 7th Session, November 17, a.m., 1961, p. 2.

[76]"My own Committee looks with pride upon the fact that it offered the idea for the OECD and sees it now come into fruition. It is an initiative that has already earned the thanks of the whole Atlantic Community for the NATO Parliamentarians' Conference"--Sen. Javits in ibid., 6th Session, November 25, 1960, p. 48. See also his statement that Douglas Dillon had "attributed the idea" of an OECD to the Atlantic Congress.

[77]NPC, Senate Report, op. cit., 5th Session, November 16-20, 1959, p. 6.

[78]NPC, op. cit., 7th Session, November 13-17, 1961, p. 57. See also Lord Crathorne, NPC, Verbatim Report, op. cit., 7th Session, November 16, a.m., 1961, p. 15.

[79]NPC, op. cit., p. 42, and Lord Crathorne, op. cit.

[80]See section above on the Economic Committee.

[81]See section above on the Political Committee, and U. S. Senate, Fourth NATO Parliamentarians' Conference, op. cit., p. 7.

program, the NATO Advanced Study Institute and a NATO Research Program;[82] the office the the NATO Science Adviser.[83]

Unfortunately, it is seldom possible to demonstrate that a particular result in this field is directly and primarily attributable to a single source. The NPC's "case" is the strongest with respect to the NATO science programs, the Atlantic Congress, the Atlantic Convention of NATO Nations, the Atlantic Institute, and the Atlantic Community Development Group for Latin America. Only in those instances would the claim to a decisive role appear to be supported in some measure by the existence of both a timely, concrete recommendation for action (as distinct from a general endorsement of principle) and evidence of active follow-up efforts by the Conference or its individual participants.

The larger and more fundamental concerns of the Conference have fared less well. The NPC has deplored in vain the failure of the governments to attain what it regarded as acceptable minimum force levels, adequate standards of political consultation, the proper degree of military supply integration, or a satisfactory measure of common effort in the fields of atomic strategy, scientific research, and public information.

It is hardly surprising, then, that the Conference has manifested a growing concern over the courteous unresponsiveness of NATO and the national governments to its ideas, and has taken a number of steps both to improve its internal arrangements and to examine the pros and cons of acquiring official status.

To be sure, although these steps have been voted in most cases without dissent, it would be mistaken to suppose that all NATO Parliamentarians are eager to reform the organization. The ability of an international parliamentary assembly to get its recommendations translated into action, as has been pointed out above,[84] is only one of several possible standards

[82]NPC, op. cit., 6th Session, November 21-26, 1960, p. 19-20; see also the section above on the Scientific and Technical Committee.

[83]NPC, Summary Report, Meeting of the Scientific and Technical Committee, October 6 and 7, 1961 (Dr. W. A. Nierenberg, Assistant Secretary General for Scientific Affairs, NATO), p. 1.

[84]Chapter 1.

of evaluation. A number of NATO parliamentarians are inclined to put greater emphasis on the importance of other values — the personal contacts, the interplay of national viewpoints, the informality of relations with top officials of NATO and its military commands. By no means all members of the NATO Parliamentarians' Conference want to transform it into a more efficient, harder-working body with more formal procedures, longer sessions, bigger staff, more money, and the more extensive personal commitments all this would entail for the participants.

The Conference as a whole, nevertheless, appears committed to a continuing effort to increase its efficiency, prestige and influence as a factor in Atlantic cooperation.

The principal causes of the parliamentarians' frustration have been the inability to obtain adequate pertinent information; the failure of the NATO Council and Secretary General either to implement or to comment on most Conference proposals; the unresponsiveness of the member governments to most NPC recommendations; and the paucity of operating funds, with consequent restrictions on staffing, travel and frequency of committee meetings.

There is no doubt that official status, when and if it becomes politically attainable, would make all of those problems more tractable. Indeed — although, as the Strasbourg experience demonstrates,[85] official status would hardly be a panacea — it would seem indispensable to any major improvement of the NPC operation.

The essence of an official relationship between the executive and the parliamentary organs is the existence of defined, reciprocal responsibilities. With regard, for example, to the flow of information, the reports that make the most difference to parliamentary consultation are those that may be prepared expressly for the assembly by the executive agency or agencies with which it is functionally related. If eleven years of unsuccessful effort by the NPC to extract reports of that nature from the NATO Council and Secretary General prove anything, it is that in this as in other respects, official status is a prerequisite. It is true that the Consultative Assembly and the WEU Assembly, which receive mandatory reports

---

[85]See Chapter 4.

from their respective ministerial bodies, have seldom been satisfied with those reports. They nevertheless furnish, in effect, a periodic accounting of the implementation of Assembly recommendations — or lack of it — by the governments. As such they provide the means by which, in A. H. Robertson's phrase, the governmental "power of decision exercised in private is set off against the politicians' right of criticism exercised in public." As Robertson adds, "the Ministers, who are themselves politicians, are naturally not anxious to expose themselves to more criticism than they must. As a result the powers of the Assembly to influence the Ministers are much greater than might at first appear...."[86]

Official status for an interparliamentary consultative body confers other advantages as well. In the case of the European assemblies, for example, as will be seen in the next chapter, it has given the parliamentarians greater assurance that their recommendations will be studied and acknowledged, has made possible the opportunity to put questions to ministers and obtain replies, and has provided the basis for the prerogative of voting motions to disagree or even to censure.

Official status for an assembly is likely, as a practical matter, to have the further advantage of assuring a more nearly adequate budget. The annual budgets of the Consultative Assembly of the Council of Europe and of the European Parliament are in the neighborhood of $5 million each, in contrast to the $220,000 available to the NATO Parliamentarians' Conference. Even the Assembly of Western European Union, with less than half the NPC membership and a far narrower functional scope, has nearly twice the financial resources.

Pending eventual attainment of official status, the Conference has necessarily fallen back on piecemeal reforms. If the Standing Committee's recent efforts to obtain national commitments for an increased budget are pursued and eventually prove successful, there will be new possibilities for improving the effectiveness of the Conference within the limits of its present quasi-official standing.

---

[86]A. H. Robertson, The Council of Europe: Its Structure, Functions and Achievements (New York: Frederick A. Praeger, Inc., 1956), p. 214.

One of the urgent needs, for example, is to augment the staff. A strengthened secretariat could remedy the present deficiencies of conference-servicing and documentation, about which a number of parliamentarians have complained. It would also permit the preparation of more effective reports and recommendations. It is perhaps no coincidence that a disproportionate share of the concrete achievements of the Conference in respect of resolutions implemented grew out of projects in which American legislators — who enjoy far more adequate staff assistance than do most of their European associates — took a predominant interest.

An augmented budget would also facilitate certain reforms of structure and method. These might include special arrangements, as will be suggested in Chapter 9, to obtain competent annual reviews and analyses of Atlantic issues. They might also include measures to provide a systematic follow-up of resolutions and recommendations. The Consultative Assembly has pioneered some highly effective follow-up techniques, and these might well be adapted to the purposes of the NATO Parliamentarians' Conference.[87]

Such reforms of staffing, structure and procedures would heighten the impact of the Conference on public opinion and governmental policy, but the full potential of the organization will not be reached unless and until it attains official status.

---

[87]See Chapter 5.

CHAPTER **4** THE
EUROPEAN
ASSEMBLIES

Any serious attempt to bring Western parliamentarians
into a more productive relationship with the processes of
Atlantic regional cooperation must take due note of the experience of Europe's three principal parliamentary consultative bodies — the Consultative Assembly of the Council of
Europe, the Assembly of Western European Union, and the
European Parliament.

In the first place, their procedures and structures, and
their relations with executive agencies, considered in the light
of their substantive achievements and failures, offer important insights into how and how not to organize interparliamentary consultation. In the second place, as noted in Chapter 1,
those three assemblies, together with the NATO Parliamentarians' Conference, present a picture of overlapping purposes, powers, methods and membership that would appear
both undesirable and, theoretically, avoidable. The four
assemblies collectively are therefore the object of a variety
of proposals for rationalization.

THE CONSULTATIVE ASSEMBLY OF THE
COUNCIL OF EUROPE

In respect of aims, composition, functions and powers,
the Consultative Assembly of the Council of Europe has more
in common with the NATO Parliamentarians' Conference than
do the other European parliamentary assemblies. Their
points of similarity and difference are therefore of particular interest.

Origins and Establishment

The Council of Europe was created by a treaty that entered
into force on August 3, 1949. The original signatories were

the Brussels Treaty Powers — Great Britain, France, Belgium, the Netherlands and Luxembourg — plus Denmark, Ireland, Italy, Norway and Sweden. The following countries joined later: Greece and Turkey (1949), Iceland (1950), German Federal Republic (March 1950 — full status in May 1951), Austria (1956), Switzerland (1963), Cyprus (1963). The Saar participated, as an associate member, from March 1950 to January 1, 1957. The Council's origins are traceable directly to the proposals and pressures of the nongovernmental European Movement. Its structure is the result of a compromise, essentially, between the views of the British Labour Government and those of the Continental federalists, under which a Consultative Assembly deliberating in public and authorized to initiate recommendations was offset by a Committee of Ministers meeting in private and authorized to determine which recommendations might be submitted to the governments.

Internal Arrangements

The purpose of the Council of Europe, as set forth in Article 1 of the Statute, is "to achieve greater unity between its Members" with a view to safeguarding their common ideals and "facilitating their economic and social progress." The methods for achieving those aims are "discussion of questions of common concern" and "agreements and common action in economic, social, cultural, scientific, legal and administrative matters."

The Committee of Ministers, in which each Member has one representative and one vote, was given powers that have been aptly described as "wide in scope but narrow in effect."[1] The Committee is to "consider the action required to further the aim of the Council of Europe" and to communicate its "conclusions" to the Member governments (Article 15). If the conclusions take the form of recommendations, there must be a unanimous vote of those present and voting, and those voting must comprise a majority of the membership (Article 20). The Committee thus lacks both a precise, positive mandate and the power to commit its governments even by unanimous vote. In practice the initiative for ideas and proposals has been exercised almost solely by the Assembly, with the Committee then deciding what to do about them. The relationship

---

[1]A. H. Robertson, European Institutions (London: Stevens & Sons, 1959), p. 62. See also A. H. Robertson, The Council of Europe, op. cit.; and European Organisations, op. cit., Chap. 4.

between the two has inevitably been an unhappy one. The Committee's principal obligation toward the Assembly is to furnish the latter at each session with "statements of its activities, accompanied by appropriate documentation" (Article 19).

The Consultative Assembly is empowered to "discuss and make recommendations upon any matter within the aim and scope of the Council of Europe" (Article 23). During its first two years, the Assembly proposed extensive revisions of the Statute with a view to making the Council "a European political authority with limited functions but real powers."[2] Having failed to obtain governmental agreement on that objective, the Assembly turned to more modest and more successful endeavors, notably the instigation of intergovernmental conventions and, starting in 1953, the holding of debates on major political questions.

As regards the internal operation of the Council, the Assembly was able during the first two years to obtain several concessions from the Committee of Ministers in the direction of increased authority: the requirement of the Statute that its agenda be approved by the Committee of Ministers was abolished; the Assembly's committees obtained the right to meet between rather than merely during sessions — they now meet at various times throughout the year for an average of one week at a time; the Statute was amended to provide that Representatives to the Assembly be chosen not by the governments but by the national parliaments or appointed in such manner as the latter may decide; the Committee of Ministers agreed to consult the Assembly before inviting additional states to join the Council; notwithstanding the provision of Article 1 (d) that "matters relating to national defense do not fall within the scope of the Council of Europe," the Assembly early and successfully asserted its right to deal with the "political" aspects of European defense.[3]

---

[2]Council of Europe, Consultative Assembly, 1st Session, September 6, 1949, Doc. 87, p. 7.

[3]See esp. Council of Europe, Resolution adopted by the Committee of Ministers at its Eighth Session, Strasbourg, May and August 1951, which deals with the admission of new members, the preparation of conventions, coordination between the Ministers and the Assembly, the creation of Specialized Authorities, and relations with intergovernmental and nongovernmental international organizations; and ibid., Resolution on Partial Agreements, August 1951, 9th Session of Committee of Ministers, quoted in Second Supplementary Report of the Committee of Ministers, Doc. 60, November 26, 1951, p. 573.

The Representatives to the Assembly, as noted above, are now chosen by the parliaments or are appointed in such manner as the latter may stipulate. They must be nationals but need not be M.P.'s of their countries (though they almost invariably are) and may not be at the same time members of the Committee of Ministers (Article 25). Ministers may sit and speak but not vote at plenary and committee meetings of the Assembly (Rule 45 of Rules of the Assembly),[4] and recently individual ministers and agency heads have begun submitting their actions and proposals to oral questions in plenary session.

The number of Representatives per Member is set forth in Article 26 on a rough basis of relative populations:

Table 2
Representation in the Consultative Assembly

	Representatives and Votes
United Kingdom France West Germany Italy	18 each
Turkey	10
Belgium Greece Netherlands	7 each
Austria Sweden Switzerland	6 each
Denmark Norway	5 each
Ireland	4
Iceland Luxembourg Cyprus	3 each
TOTAL	144

[4]Council of Europe, Procedure of the Assembly (Strasbourg, 1953). A requirement of advance authorization of the Commitee was deleted from the Committee's rules in July 1955.

The minimum of three Representatives for each of the small-
est members assures representation for all the principal
non-Communist parties. At plenary sessions of the Assembly,
the Representatives are seated alphabetically by name in
semi-circular rows facing the chair and the rostrum. The
national delegations are thus split up. The participants are
uninstructed by government, parliament or party, and they
vote as individuals. Certain enumerated actions, including
recommendations or opinions to be transmitted to the Committee of Ministers, the setting up of committees and the inclusion of items on the agenda, require a two-thirds majority
of those voting (Article 29) which must comprise at least
one-third of the Representatives of the Assembly (Rule 35).

From the outset the Assembly has drawn a distinction
between Recommendations, which are addressed to the Committee of Ministers and which call for action of some kind,
and Resolutions, which do not call for such action. Resolutions may be addressed to other agencies or a group of governments, or they may record opinions destined for the world at
large. Under Rule 35, resolutions other than those specified
in the Statute are adopted by an absolute majority of the votes
cast. These include the opinions addressed to agencies other
than the Committee of Ministers.

According to the Statute (Article 32):

The Consultative Assembly shall meet in ordinary session once a year, the date and duration of which shall
be determined by the Assembly so as to avoid as far
as possible overlapping with parliamentary sessions
of Members and with sessions of the General Assembly
of the United Nations. In no circumstances shall the
duration of an ordinary session exceed one month unless both the Assembly and the Committee of Ministers
concur.

The two organs must also agree to the calling, date and place
of extraordinary sessions. The Assembly meets in its modern,
"temporary" building at the seat of the Council, in Strasbourg,
unless the two organs agree otherwise.

A Secretary General and a staff of some 430 (which
is increased by an average of 240 during sessions of the
Assembly) serve both the Assembly and the Committee of

Ministers.[5] The Council of Europe's current annual budget
is on the order of $5,000,000.

Practice and Program

During its seventeen years of operation the Consultative
Assembly adopted more than 900 recommendations, resolutions or opinions of a substantive nature, or an average of approximately 56 per session.[6] Such an outpouring of proposals
has not produced the looked-for results, and, as will be seen
later, the Assembly has taken a series of steps, including efforts to reduce the number of resolutions, in the hope of se-
curing a more satisfactory record of implementation.

One principal activity of the Council has been the initiation
of conventions or treaties. By 1961, as the Committee of
Ministers noted in an unwontedly laudatory communication to
the Assembly, 32 European conventions and agreements had
been concluded by the Council and 25 had entered into force.
These, the Committee declared, "represent the beginnings of
a 'European legal system' in varied fields: human rights,
social security, patents, equivalence of diplomas, peaceful
settlement of disputes, extradition, establishment, public
health, abolition of passports and other measures to minimise
frontier formalities." The Committee gave credit for this
progress to the Consultative Assembly as "the driving force
of Europe ... the forum for the interchange of ideas ... the
source of constructive proposals" which "merit careful study
by the Committee of Ministers itself and by other intergovernmental agencies...."[7]

---

[5]As one close observer of international parliamentary bodies has
remarked, "It is possible that most members of the Assembly have
better staff help there than in their own national parliaments."--
Philander P. Claxton, Jr., Prospects for an Atlantic Parliamentary
Assembly, unpublished study for the Fifth Senior Seminar in Foreign
Policy, Foreign Service Institute, Department of State, June 1963, p. 12.
Source of data: letter from R. Rössler, Secretary of the Permanent
Working Party on Parliamentary and Public Relations, November 16,
1964.

[6]Council of Europe, Directorate of Information, Balance Sheet of
the Work of the Council of Europe (1949-1956), op. cit. Table II, p. 18,
supplemented by letter cited in footnote above.

[7]"Role of the Council of Europe," Communication of the Committee
of Ministers to the Consultative Assembly, January 4, 1961.

The European Convention for the Protection of Human Rights and Fundamental Freedoms is generally cited as the most notable single achievement of the Council of Europe. Signed on November 4, 1950, and put into effect on September 3, 1953, the Convention defines the rights of citizens in a democratic society[8] and provides international machinery — the European Commission of Human Rights and the European Court of Human Rights — to help protect those rights. The Commission considers complaints brought by a member government and (if the states concerned have recognized such competence) by individuals and private groups concerning violations by other members. If the Commissions' recommendations for settlement of complaints are not accepted, the Committee of Ministers may then, by two-thirds majority, issue decisions binding upon the parties. The European Court of Human Rights came into existence in 1958 when eight states accepted its compulsory jurisdiction. A. H. Robertson observes that the Convention "constituted a milestone in international law and marked a distinct advance on anything previously attempted for the international protection of human rights and the rule of law."[9]   In a sense, of course, the

---

[8]The rights defined and protected by the Convention are: the right to life; freedom from torture; freedom from slavery and servitude; the liberty and security of person; the right to a fair trial; protection against ex post facto laws; the right to privacy; freedom of thought, conscience and religion; freedom of expression; freedom of assembly and association; the right to marry; the right to an effective remedy against the violation of such rights. In March 1952 a protocol was signed extending these rights to include the peaceful enjoyment of property, the right to education and to free elections at reasonable intervals by secret ballot. See Council of Europe, The European Convention on Human Rights (Strasbourg: 1952); Robertson, op. cit.; P.E.P., European Organizations, op. cit., p. 154-155; Gordon L. Weil, The European Convention on Human Rights (Leyden: A. W. Sythoff, 1963).

[9]European Institutions, op. cit., p. 68. Cf. Gordon L. Weil, "The Evolution of the European Convention on Human Rights," American Journal of International Law, Vol. 57, No. 4, October 1963. As of October 1963, more than 1500 applications had been submitted to the Commission. Of these only 14 — 11 from individuals and all three received from member states — were declared admissible. --Ibid., p. 809; Egon Schwelb, "On the Operation of the European Convention on Human Rights," International Organization, Vol. XVIII, No. 3, Summer 1964, p. 558-585; A. H. Robertson, Human Rights in Europe (Dobbs Ferry, N.Y.: Oceana Publications, Inc., 1963).

Convention did not so much achieve an advance as record a consensus at a particular historical conjuncture. The Commission and the Court have had little "business" of significance. Not all of the member states have acknowledged the competence of the Commission in regard to individual complaints or accepted the compulsory jurisdiction of the Court. With respect to those states that did accept it, there is no means of enforcement against any that might choose to ignore a decision or disregard an obligation. As a practical matter, the Convention is less an instrument for the international protection of human rights threatened by state policy than a reflection of the rights the adhering states are determined to protect and are willing to expose to international legal scrutiny. As a legal matter, the Convention did set important new international standards for the protection of human rights.

The Consultative Assembly has developed its influence in two other areas of European concern, and its activities there may well be more important, if less susceptible to precise evaluation, than its achievements in the realm of technical intergovernmental conventions. It has gained or assumed a measure of parliamentary supervision or criticism over the activities of numerous intergovernmental agencies affecting Western Europe;[10] and it has asserted some measure of public opinion leadership in issues of foreign policy and European integration.

The Assembly established its role as a leader of public opinion in 1953, when it took up and debated "the policy of the Council of Europe in the light of recent developments in the international situation." The discussion was aimed at the then impending four-power conference in Berlin. Forty-eight representatives from thirteen countries, led off by Spaak, took part in the debate. As Sir Anthony Nutting told the House of Commons later, "It is no exaggeration to say that both the debate that ensued and the resolution which the Assembly subsequently passed did a great deal to raise and hearten European morale at an important time and to give renewed impetus to European defense policy.... This debate raised the standing of the Assembly, and, indeed, of the Council of Europe, more than any other discussion in the four years of

---

[10] E.g., OECD, Western European Union, European Coal and Steel Community, European Conference of Ministers of Transport, European Civil Aviation Conference and certain specialized agencies of the United Nations.

its existence."[11] In December 1953 the Committee of Ministers was moved by that performance to "express its earnest hope that the Assembly will continue to debate major political questions of this kind, thus affording guidance to European public opinion."[12]

Such debates have since become a regular feature of the Assembly. They have proved of particular significance in regard to specific problems of European integration that arose between "the Six" and the "non-Six." To that forum the ministers of each have journeyed at moments of crisis in European affairs to define and justify their policies and to seek parliamentary and public support for them. The process has served to clarify the issues and, at certain junctures, to influence developments.

It was at Strasbourg, for example, that most continental advocates of European unity were usefully disabused of their belief that Britain would in effect join the Six once the Labour Government had been replaced. The speech to the Assembly by Home Secretary Sir David Maxwell Fyfe after the Conservatives returned to power in October 1951 was a landmark — or at least a major detour sign — in the evolution of European integration. To the continentals, his inability to "promise you that our eventual association with the European Defense Community will amount to full and unconditional participation" and his statement that Britain would only "enter into relations" with the Coal and Steel Community[13] were a bitter disappointment. The disappointment was the greater because Winston Churchill, in a previous session, had been a prime mover of the proposal for a European army and, in the House of Commons, had strongly attacked the Labour Government for having refused to join the Schuman Plan negotiations. It was at last fully clear that the continentals would have to proceed — for the time being — without Britain.

Other debates have been of comparable utility. All of the main continental initiatives for unification were of course

---

[11]House of Commons Debate, October 23, 1953, col. 2321.

[12]Council of Europe, Consultative Assembly, Communication of the Committee of Ministers, Doc. 220, January 8, 1954, p. 1.

[13]Council of Europe, Consultative Assembly, Official Record of Debates, 3d Session, November 28, 1951, p. 513-514.

fully and early aired in the Consultative Assembly, with considerable effect in terms of public and parliamentary support. As André Philip has written, "There is no doubt that for President Schuman the fact of having gone before the Consultative Assembly and having obtained its approval of his plan was a decisive factor in the creation of the Coal and Steel Community. It was likewise at Strasbourg, in connection with a debate on Germany and a reply to a report of the Committee of Ministers, where for the first time there appeared the idea of establishing a European Defense Community."[14]

A review of two other debates will perhaps suffice to point up the value of a consultative assembly, particularly in a creative phase of international community development such as that of Western Europe in the 1950's. By mid-1952 the Coal and Steel Community was a going concern; the Contractual Agreement had been signed, thus ending the occupation of West Germany and paving the way for German participation in Western defense; the treaty had been concluded for establishment of the European Defense Community; and preparations were being made to draft the statute of a European Political Authority. With these developments, the pressure on Britain, emanating in part from Strasbourg, to define its policy toward Europe, and to do so in as constructive a fashion as possible, had brought Foreign Secretary Anthony Eden to the Assembly for a speech that marked a definite turning point in British policy. His purpose was to refute widespread charges of what the London Economist and others had identified as official British uneasiness regarding "the prospect of a tightly-knit and exclusive community growing up across the Channel,"[15] and to reassure the Six that the "Eden Plan," proposed the preceding March, was intended not to give Britain power without responsibility but only to provide useful links between the Six and the Fifteen.[16] The Foreign Secretary's statement represented a reversal rather than a "clarification" of policy. It was adopted in the face of

---

[14]André Philip, L'Europe unie et sa place dans l'économie internationale, op. cit., p. 314.

[15]September 13, 1952, p. 607.

[16]Council of Europe, Consultative Assembly, Official Report of Debates, 4th Session, Vol. III, September 15, 1952, p. 281-282. The Eden Plan will be considered below, in connection with other "multiple-tier" proposals for international parliamentary reorganization.

certain _faits accomplis_ and under pressure that had been engendered in important part at Strasbourg.[17]

In September 1954 another "European" debate took place in the Assembly, this one prompted by the French rejection of the EDC Treaty. The debate occurred shortly before the London Conference out of which the Brussels Treaty Organization was reborn as Western European Union. More than fifty speakers took part in the formulation of a Council consensus that was expressed in an important declaration. The effects were, as always, impossible to evaluate precisely, but Harold Macmillan later told the Assembly: "No one can ever over-estimate the immense contribution toward the final ratification of those agreements by the debates in this Assembly in the autumn of last year."[18]

THE ASSEMBLY OF WESTERN EUROPEAN UNION

The Assembly of Western European Union came into being, in the words of a leading participant, as "an afterthought." It was designed mainly to meet the desire of some governments to have a parliamentary body associated with German

---

[17]For an analysis of that policy change see J. Allan Hovey, Jr., "Britain and the Unification of Europe," International Organization, August 1955, p. 3-6. The importance of Eden's statement lay in the fact that contrary to earlier published indications, the British had abandoned any intention of compelling a choice between Little and Greater Europe. As the present writer has noted elsewhere: "Without assurance of British support, about which considerable uncertainty had been raised by British statements in past debates of the Council of Europe, important segments of continental opinion, like that led by M. Mollet, would view the undertaking of a Little Europe with greatly increased apprehension.... By the time of Eden's speech to the Assembly both the Common and the Ad Hoc Assemblies had met, and their decisions served to present Mr. Eden with a new situation. In the interim, confronted with what amounted to a _fait accompli_, he reportedly scrapped his original speech. What he substituted for it was destined to warm the hearts of the continental federalists."--American Committee on United Europe, Report from Strasbourg, January 1953, p. 12.

[18]Council of Europe, Consultative Assembly, Official Report of Debates, op. cit., 7th Session, July 6, 1955, p. 35.

rearmament.[19]   But for the objections of Sweden, according to one authority, its functions might have been assigned to the Consultative Assembly.[20]

Origins and Establishment

The rejection of the EDC Treaty by the French National Assembly in August 1954, was followed in September by a nine-power conference (the Six, Britain, Canada and the United States) which decided to make the Brussels Treaty the instrument for incorporating the Federal Republic of Germany into Western defense arrangements.[21]   Under the "Treaty of Economic, Social and Cultural Collaboration and Collective Self-Defense" signed at Brussels March 17, 1948, Britain, France and the Benelux countries had pledged each other automatic military assistance in the event any party became the object of an armed attack in Europe (Art. 4). While the treaty dealt with the contingency of any "renewal by Germany of an aggressive policy" (Art. 7 and Preamble), its primary purpose was to organize a common defense against the danger of Soviet attack. The treaty also committed the parties to cooperate economically (Art. 2), to "develop on corresponding lines the social and other related services of their countries" (Art. 2) and to promote cultural exchanges (Art. 3). A Consultative Council, established under Article 7, was to be "so organised as to be able to exercise its functions continuously."

The Protocol Modifying and Completing the Brussels Treaty was signed in Paris on October 23, 1954. It made the following changes in the original treaty: One of the purposes of the treaty, to take steps against any renewed German aggression, was replaced by the words "to promote the unity and encourage the progressive integration of Europe" (Article 2 of the Protocol); The Consultative Council was renamed

---

[19]WEU, Assembly, State of European Security, 1956-1961, 7th Session, Committee on Defence Questions and Armaments, Doc. 215, November 10, 1961, p. 9.

[20]Kenneth Lindsay, Towards a European Parliament (Strasbourg: Council of Europe, 1958), p. 20.

[21]Department of State, London and Paris Agreements, September-October 1954.

the Council of Western European Union (Art. 4); it was agreed that the treaty would be carried out in "close cooperation" with NATO (Art. 3); the WEU Assembly was established (Art. 5). Three additional Protocols were also incorporated into the treaty. Protocol II established the maximum total strength of land and air forces each party was to maintain in Europe in peacetime and set forth Britain's conditional undertaking not to withdraw its four divisions and tactical air force from Europe "against the wishes of the majority of the High Contracting Parties." Protocol III provided that West Germany would not produce on its territory any atomic, biological or chemical weapons and would, unless it received the consent of a two-thirds majority of the Council of WEU, refrain from manufacturing guided missiles, large warships or strategic bombers. Protocol IV established the Agency for the Control of Armaments with a mandate to supervise German compliance with the ban on the ABC and heavy weapons and to control the level of stocks of these weapons maintained by the other parties in Europe. A Standing Armaments Committee was established by the Council at its first meeting to promote the standardization of existing and new equipment.[22] The Council also established committees of senior civil servants — the Social Committe, the Public Health Committee, the War Pensions Committee and the Cultural Committee — which developed a number of conventions now in effect in those fields. Finally, an agreement of October 23, 1954, between France and West Germany assigned the WEU Council the task of supervising the referendum in the Saar and implementing the territory's European statute.[23]

Western Europe's third parliamentary assembly was established by the adoption of a single new article that reads as follows:

The Council of Western European Union shall make an Annual Report on its activities and in particular concerning the control of armaments to an Assembly

[22]WEU, Communiqué, First Session of the Council of Western European Union, Paris, May 7, 1955.

[23]WEU, Resolution of the Council of Western European Union on the Agreement between the Government of the Federal Republic of Germany and the Government of the French Republic on the Saar Statute, May 11, 1955.

composed of representatives of the Brussels Treaty
Powers to the Consultative Assembly of the Council of
Europe. [24]

Internal Arrangements

The Assembly is thus composed as follows:

Table 3
Representation in the Assembly of
Western European Union

	Representatives
France, West Germany, Italy, United Kingdom	18 each
Belgium, Netherlands	7 each
Luxembourg	3
TOTAL	89

The amended Brussels Treaty went into effect on May 6, 1955,
and the Assembly held its first session in July.

In view of the offhand way in which the Assembly was
created, the preparation of a "charter" became the Assembly's
first task. Both the Charter and the Rules of Procedure can
usefully be studied in connection with any proposed modification of the NATO Parliamentarians' Conference. Both documents reflect a deliberate attempt to profit from the experience of the delegates with the Statute and Rules of the Council
of Europe. As will be seen below, the differences are all in
the direction of giving the WEU Assembly greater authority,
facility and freedom. The Assembly's drafts of these documents were amended following a joint meeting between the
President of the Assembly and the Council, in which the
Council had raised certain objections. The Charter and

---

[24]Article IX of the revised treaty; Article V of the first Protocol.

Rules were adopted by the A s s e m b l y on October 24, 1955.[25]

The Charter of the Assembly, consisting of twelve articles, defines the nature and scope of the Assembly as follows (Art. I):

(a) The Assembly carries out the parliamentary function arising from the application of the Brussels Treaty.

In particular, the Assembly may proceed on any matter arising out of the Brussels Treaty and upon any matter submitted to the Assembly for an Opinion by the Council.

The Assembly meets in Strasbourg as often as its business may require, typically six to eight days a year, immediately before and after sessions of the Consultative Assembly of the Council of Europe (Art. III). Unlike the latter, the WEU Assembly can be convened in extraordinary session by the President without the consent of the executive body (Art. III-b).

The Assembly is empowered under Article V-a to "make Recommendations or transmit Opinions to the Council on any matter consonant with the aims and falling within the terms of reference of Western European Union," and it makes a formal "reply" to the Report of the Council (Art. V-g).

Unlike the Consultative Assembly, the WEU delegates established control over their agenda from the outset. Under Article I-b, the agenda is limited only by the scope of the Brussels Treaty and by a "due regard to the activities of other European organisations." Since the Treaty embraces the aims of European unity, and economic, social and cultural collaboration, the WEU Assembly's competence (without regard to its role in collective self-defense) is as broad as that of the Consultative Assembly.

The importance of taking into account "the activities of other European organisations" is therefore evident, but it had been thought that the danger of overlap would be obviated

---

[25]WEU Secretariat, Charter and Rules of Procedure of the Assembly of Western European Union, 1957. See also WEU Secretariat, Assembly of Western European Union, Practice and Procedure, July 1958. Another particularly useful source is A. H. Robertson, European Institutions, op. cit., p. 126-147.

by the provision that participants in the smaller body must be the Members' representatives in the Consultative Assembly. The WEU Assembly's original intention, moreover, was to maintain a clear-cut division of work. As the Rapporteur of the Committee on Organization told the Assembly:

> The essential point here is that, in principle, armaments questions and the Saar will receive their parliamentary discussion in this Assembly, other matters in the Consultative Assembly. Thus, the cultural, social and economic activities of the Council of WEU will be given parliamentary scrutiny and support first in the Consultative Assembly and its appropriate Committees. We shall thus avoid the same members of parliament considering the same issues twice over in different Committee rooms. [26]

A loophole, however, was provided by Article V-c of the Charter:

> The report from the Council on the activities of Western European Union in other spheres dealt with in the annual report transmitted to the Consultative Assembly shall be considered by the Western European Union Assembly in cases where this is considered necessary.

Moreover, after the Saar Referendum had terminated one of its major functions, the Assembly decided in April 1956 to establish a General Affairs Committee to deal with social and cultural matters. Thereafter, neither good intentions nor identity of membership were enough to prevent some duplication of work. Repeated and only partly successful efforts in the ensuing two years to eliminate it culminated in April 1959 in a decision of the Foreign Ministers concerned to transfer the social and economic activities of Western European Union to the Council of Europe. [27]

---

[26] WEU Assembly, Proceedings, 1st Session, October 1955, Doc. 3, p. 177.

[27] The decision was based on a recommendation of a Special Committee named by the Council of Europe's Committee of Ministers to study a memorandum by Pierre Wigny, the Belgian Foreign Minister. These developments are recounted in Ten Years of the Council of Europe (Strasbourg: 1960), p. 14-15. The Wigny memorandum appears in WEU Assembly, Presidential Committee, Rationalisation of European Institutions other than those of the Six, Text of the Aide-Memoire transmitted by the Belgian Government to the Member States of the Council of Europe, February 6, 1959 -- Doc. A/WEU/CP(59)6, May 15, 1959. Cf. Robertson, op. cit., p. 140-142.

Again as distinct from its Strasbourg forebear, the WEU Assembly successfully asserted its right (Art. VIII) to draw up its own budget (which is then subject to Council approval) and to appoint its own secretariat (Art. IX). The Assembly registered another gain when it provided that the official languages of all Members would be simultaneously interpreted into the other official languages (Art. X). (Speakers addressing the Council of Europe Assembly in other than English and French are responsible for arranging for consecutive interpretation into one of the official languages, which is then simultaneously rendered in the other official language.) WEU documents are normally published only in English and French, but Rule 19 provides that documents of the Assembly and its committees "possessing exceptional public interest shall be published" in other languages "if the Assembly so decides" — a provision of considerable potential value when it comes to follow-up procedures at the national level.

The Charter and Rules record a number of interesting steps designed to establish greater accountability of the Council to the Assembly. Thus the Assembly went as far as it reasonably could toward conferring on itself a right of censure. Article V-h states:

A motion to disagree to the content of the report, or to a part of the report, shall be tabled in writing by at least ten Representatives.

The adoption of such a motion, which shall not be put to the vote until at least 24 hours after it has been tabled, shall require a majority of the Representatives to the Assembly.

This provision was inspired by Article 25 of the Rules of what is now the European Parliament, under which a motion of censure supported by two-thirds of the membership can overthrow an executive agency of the Community. This rule, like that of the WEU, is a prefiguration of the parliamentary vote of no confidence. It has been reported[28] that the WEU ministers were particularly unhappy about it, notwithstanding indications that it was expected to be used not so much against the Council as against the heads of its executive agencies. The ministers were able however to obtain only one modification in the Assembly's original draft, a clause indicating

---

[28]A. H. Robertson, European Institutions, op. cit., p. 142-143.

that the motion to disagree must be germane to the Council report. The practical effect of a resolution to disagree, as the Defense Committee has observed, would lie in the influence such a public disavowal might have "on opinion, in particular in national parliaments."[29]

In the same vein, Article V-e, which sets forth the powers of the Assembly, provides that the committees[30] "may formulate questions, which shall be transmitted by the President of the Assembly to the Council" and:

A reply may be postponed or omitted for reasons of European interest. The text of the questions put to the Council and of the replies thereto shall be included in the preliminary reports of the Committees to the Assembly.

Similar treatment is provided in Article V-i and Rule 45 for questions from individual Representatives, and it is further stipulated (Rule 45-2) that "All questions governed by this rule to which an answer has not been given within a period of one month shall be published, together with a statement that no reply was received." Provision is also made, subject to approval of the Council, for the establishment of Assembly "Committees of investigation" (Art. VII-f) and for the committees to hear officials of WEU and its subsidiary bodies (Art. VII-e).

The voting requirements, set forth in Article V-g and Rule 35, are also more flexible than those of the Consultative Assembly. Rule 35 states:

(a) for the amendment of the Charter and for adoption of a motion to disagree to the Annual Report, or to any

---

[29] State of European Security 1955-1961, op. cit., p. 10. Only one such motion has been submitted -- in May 1957, with respect to the reduction of British forces on the Continent. It failed of a two-thirds majority. -- WEU Assembly, 10th Session, Application of Brussels Treaty, Committee on Defense Questions and Armaments (Georges Housciaux, Belgium: Rapporteur), Doc. 309, April 24, 1964, p. 8.

[30] The committees as stipulated in the 1957 edition of Rules are: Committee on Defense Questions and Armaments, General Affairs Committee, Committee on Budgetary Affairs and Administration, Committee on Rules of Procedure and Privileges.

part of the Report: a majority of the Representatives
to the Assembly;

(b) for any other decision: an absolute majority of the
votes cast;

(c) for appointments, subject to the provisions of Rule
10 above [concerning the Bureau]: an absolute majority
of votes cast at the first ballot and a relative majority
at the second ballot.

Thus, from the point of view of the parliamentarian, the
procedures and powers of the WEU Assembly represent a
distinct advance over those of the Consultative Assembly.

Practice and Program

The WEU Assembly is the only European parliamentary
body to have official responsibility in the field of Western
defense, and its practice, as well as its powers and procedure,
will be pertinent to any reorganization of Atlantic parliamentary consultation.

The experience of the Assembly has been characterized
by an unremitting and only partly successful struggle with
the WEU Council to win recognition of the consultative and
supervisory functions it has asserted in the field of European
defense and to obtain enough information and cooperation
from the executive agencies to enable it to perform those
functions adequately.

By the end of 1951, the defense planning and command
responsibilities of the Brussels Treaty Organization had been
transferred to NATO. This left the Council of Western European Union, in its own view, with competence limited to:
matters to be raised by the contracting parties, notably under
Article VIII of the Brussels Treaty (settlement of disputes);
the level of forces of Member States (Protocol II); the maintenance of the British forces on the Continent as set forth in
Protocol II; the Agency for the Control of Armaments (Protocol IV); and the Standing Armaments Committee for equipment
standardization. The Assembly, while conceding that those
de facto limits on the Council's activities were necessary to
avoid duplicating the work of NATO, argued that the Council
could not abandon its competence (as distinct from the exercise

of its competence) in the broad field of European defense, particularly in view of Article V, which provides for automatic military aid against an armed attack. Accordingly, since there was no official NATO Assembly, the WEU Assembly had the right and (under Article I of its Charter) the duty to consider "the whole range of western defence, insofar as this affects the security of any member State of Western European Union. In practice this means no aspect of western defence is entirely outside the competence of the Assembly."[31]

These conflicting interpretations have never been reconciled. The Council, at the ambassadorial level, has held one or two joint meetings a year with the Assembly's Committee on Defence Questions and Armaments. In cooperation with NATO, the Council worked out a procedure by which Assembly questions falling outside the Council's competence would be referred to NATO, whose answers would be transmitted in meetings between the Council Chairman and the Committee, with NATO representatives attending as expert advisers. The first such meeting under that procedure occurred in March 1958. An Assembly Committee report comments that, "In general these joint meetings must be regarded as a useful institution, not so much for the information which they have so far provided, but for the collective responsibility of the Council to the Assembly, which they emphasise."[32]

The Assembly has made a number of proposals for improving this arrangement. One would be to harmonize the composition of the WEU and NATO Councils at the level of the permanent WEU Council, which now consists of the ambassadors of the Six in London plus a representative of the British Foreign Office. The result would be to give the Assembly an executive opposite number consisting of the representatives of the seven WEU states in the North Atlantic Council. Such a body, the Committee has argued, would be both more cognizant of defense matters and better equipped to determine the limits of security. Other Assembly suggestions for improving the value of the joint meetings have been: attendance by

---

[31]State of European Security, 1955–61, op. cit., p. 12. Cf. esp. WEU Assembly, 3d Session, Responsibility of Western European Union in the Field of Military Policy, Committee on Defence Questions and Armaments (E. de la Vallée Poussin, Rapporteur), Doc. 63, September 21, 1957.

[32]Ibid., p. 14.

one or more Defense Ministers, more active participation by the NATO advisers, and attendance of Member Countries' Permanent Representatives to NATO. [33]

None of these proposals has been implemented, and the Assembly has had to rely on other methods of obtaining the information it needed to perform what it considers its primary function. The most useful of these methods have been the appearances, since 1959, of Defense Ministers at closed meetings of the Committee; visits of inspection to Supreme Headquarters, Allied Powers in Europe and its various army, naval and air commands; the device under Article V of the Charter by which written questions are submitted by the Assembly and answered by the Council in its Annual Reports; statements (sometimes given off the record) to the plenary Assembly by the NATO Secretary General, by top allied military commanders and since 1960 by various Ministers of Defense. The Assembly has been handicapped by a ruling of the North Atlantic Council in 1958 that only unclassified information could be communicated to parliamentarians. The Defense Committee has described this an an affront to the Assembly, inconsistent with the arrangements between national parliaments and their governments, and unwarranted in view both of the Assembly's internal security and of the largely non-technical nature of the information it requires.[34]

Of the some 90 recommendations voted by the Assembly since its establishment, about one-half have concerned defense questions. Few of the latter, which cover much the

---

[33]Ibid., and Doc. 62, 3d Session, The Unification of European Assemblies, Report of General Affairs Committee (J. M. van der Goes van Naters, Rapporteur), September 21, 1957. The Rapporteur proposed that if a unified European Assembly is established, its competence and powers should include: (1) constitutional relations with a Council of Prime Ministers and departmental ministers incorporating the right to refer back a report by motion to disagree; (2) a procedure to ensure regular consideration in national parliaments of the chief recommendations (in May 1957 the President of the Assembly had raised the possibility of having European proposals receive approval in national parliaments by means of a procedure analogous to that of a "negative resolution"--ibid., p. 5); (3) with a view in part to reducing the number of draft resolutions, the establishment of a highly qualified Research Department for the committees; (4) maximal financial autonomy. --Resolution 20 adopted October 12, 1957, Doc. 79, p. 69.

[34]State of European Security, op. cit., p. 16.

same ground as do those of the NATO Parliamentarians' Military Committee, appear to have affected official action. The Assembly remains dissatisfied with the measure of co-operation and response it has received from the Council. In its basic area, arms control, its recommendations have been largely disregarded by the governments.[35]

The Assembly's main claim to success lies in the area not of substantive resolutions implemented, although there are instances of such,[36] but of strengthening parliamentary and public understanding and support of the Western defense effort. Despite the limited access to official data, reports of the Defense Committee have provided, as one observer has

---

[35]A Recommendation adopted by the Assembly on June 4, 1963, for example, protests that "the provisions of the Treaty regarding the levels of forces and the control of armaments, particularly nuclear weapons, are still not applied in accordance with the Treaty, ..." that the United Kingdom is not adhering to its commitment regarding the strength of its forces on the Continent, and that the failure of France and Italy to ratify the "due process" convention signed in Paris on December 14, 1957, is preventing the Arms Control Agency from fulfilling its duties "in the manner prescribed by the Treaty."--Recommendation 93, 10th Session, Doc. 309, April 24, 1964, p. 9. As the Explanatory Memorandum notes, "Until the Convention comes into force, the inspectors of the Agency have to give advance warning in order to gain access to the installations subject to control by the Agency and their visits will continue to be made only with the prior agreement of the authorities concerned." With regard to nuclear weapons, the memorandum explains that "the Council has never authorised the Agency for Control of Armaments to prepare the control measures in the nuclear field provided for in the Treaty, nor even to recruit qualified experts." (Ibid., p. 6.) Thus, all the nuclear provisions of the Treaty — requiring verification of the non-production of nuclear weapons or of fissile material for that purpose in Germany and verification of the level of stocks of nuclear weapons France will be permitted by the Council to maintain — remain, in the Defence Committee's phrase, "a dead letter." (Ibid., p. 7.) The Assembly's exhortations in regard to equipment standardization have largely met a similar fate.

[36]E.g., Recommendation 67, urging ratification of the convention on the "rule of law" with respect to arms control, has been credited by J.-M. Le Breton, former Clerk Assistant of the WEU Assembly, with hastening ratification in some member countries. Another example cited by the same source was the Assembly's role in promoting a reorganization of regional commands in the Baltic.

commented, "the most searching evaluations of the NATO defence system yet published."[37] As the Committee itself has stated, its reports "are widely quoted and have become a recognised source for those concerned with western defence."[38]

In the course of considering its own operating problems and the possibilities of reform, the WEU Assembly has formulated a number of propositions regarding the importance and role of an international defense assembly. One of these is that, in the words of an early report of the Defense Committee, "Since the defence of Europe was entrusted to <u>international</u> organs, parliamentary supervision of defence can no longer be effectively assured by national Parliaments alone."[39] It would clearly be more efficient to have a single international group of parliamentarians, e.g., a defense subcommittee, review and report on the work of NATO and its commands than to have representatives of national legislative committees do so separately. Moreover, while the national legislatures have the only effective parliamentary control over defense expenditures, their view is apt to be less comprehensive than that of a regional assembly. An international defense committee can help them achieve a better perspective. Parliamentary activity at the two levels is thus complementary. On this reasoning, the WEU Assembly has urged that it be given advisory powers with respect to the NATO budget and, as will be seen below, has examined a number of proposals looking toward establishment of a NATO-wide defense assembly.

Another vital aspect of an international defense assembly, one report has suggested, is that it makes "a direct

---

[37]<u>European Organisations</u> (London: Political and Economic Planning, 1959), p. 217. Cf. John Edwards, late Labour M.P. and President of Consultative Assembly: "When I am asked to justify the existence of Western European Union, I always refer to the Defence Committee.... I know of no person from whom one could obtain so well summarized and admirable marshalling of the facts and arguments concerning European defence as from Colonel Fens in his successive Reports."--WEU Assembly, <u>Proceedings</u>, 4th Session, 1st Part, Minutes, July 1958, p. 73-74.

[38]<u>State of European Security, 1955-1961</u>, op. cit., p. 10-11.

[39]WEU Assembly, <u>Responsibility of Western European Union in the field of military policy</u>, Doc. 63, <u>op. cit.</u>, p. 4.

contribution to the credibility of the western deterrent."[40]
This it is thought to do by developing among parliamentarians
of the allied countries a degree of mutual understanding and
confidence comparable to that prevailing within the executive
and command agencies. On this point Colonel Fens has
written:[41]

> As a result of [the Assembly's] efforts between 1955
> and 1961, more than 250 members of parliament from
> the seven member States have come to know each
> other as individuals, and have understood, better than
> they would have in any other way, not only the par-
> ticular problems of each country, but the strength of
> the common resolve.... When they have returned to
> their national parliaments, these members have taken
> an important part in defence debates, and now the go-
> vernments can count upon a solid nucleus of opinion
> which has learnt to look at the problem in a genuine
> western perspective.
>
> This is a revolutionary development and has re-
> ceived far too little attention. We have only to recall
> that the Rome Treaty would never have been ratified
> unless there had been in each of the parliaments a
> similar body of opinion prepared to support the ad-
> venture of a European Economic Community. Hither-
> to, it had not existed. That it does today is a tribute
> to the importance of the European assemblies.
>
> The master stroke of the Assembly of Western Eur-
> opean Union was to apply this same technique to buttres-
> sing the Alliance, and the most discerning are grateful
> for this support from an international institution, fore-
> shadowing as it does perhaps, the creation of a Western
> Defence Assembly which would play a similar role in
> grouping the European and American partners of the
> Alliance.

Since the interruption of the negotiations for British entry
into the European Communities in January 1963, there has

---

[40]WEU Assembly, The Future Organisation of Western Defence on
the Executive and Parliamentary Levels, Committee on Defence Questions and Armaments (F. J. Goedhart, Netherlands, and General Raffaele
Cadorna, Rapporteurs), Doc. 231, May 3, 1962, p. 29.

[41]State of European Security, 1955-1961, op. cit., p. 8-9.

been renewed interest in Western European Union as a "meeting place" for political and economic consultation between Britain and the Six. In July 1963 the seven governments agreed on the principle of resuming the quarterly meetings of the WEU Council at the ministerial level, the last of which had been held more than a year previously, in April 1962. The first of the "new style" meetings was held at The Hague in October 1963. An intensification of WEU activity, which had been repeatedly urged by the Assembly,[42] is generally seen as a means of promoting, as a 1964 draft recommendation of the General Affairs Committee has put it, "a rapprochement between the European Economic Community, on the one hand, and the United Kingdom and EFTA on the other, with a view to enlarging the Community."[43]

To that end a number of suggestions have been made for strengthening WEU machinery. On December 5, 1963, the Assembly recommended that the Council:

1. Improve the functioning of the permanent Council by... (a) appointment of permanent representatives responsible for the operation of the permanent Council, (b) regrouping of the permanent national delegations insofar as possible in the same premises as the Secretariat-General;

2. Appoint as Secretary-General of WEU, after consulting the Presidential Committee of the Assembly, a leading political personality with the necessary qualifications;

3. Arrange for the Secretary-General to be provided with more effective assistance... by authorising him to reorganise his service... to include: (a) creation of services for political and economic affairs and co-operation with international organisations, (b) creation of a division responsible for defence questions under the Assistant Secretary-General.[44]

---

[42]E.g., Recommendations 92, 94, 95 and 311.

[43]WEU Assembly, 10th Session, Co-ordination of the Economic Policies of the Seven, General Affairs Committee (Hubert Leynen, Belgium, Rapporteur), Doc. 312, June 9, 1964, p. 1.

[44]WEU Assembly, 9th Session, Recommendation 103, Doc. 311, p. 15. Explanatory memorandum in Doc. 291.

The Council has rejected these suggestions as inappropriate to WEU's present responsibilities.[45]

A leading British newspaper has accused Whitehall of casting a shadow over the renewed WEU contacts by making a "regular attempt at strengthening the WEU in such a way that would virtually get Britain into the Common Market through the back door."[46] The desire to see Britain join the European Communities is evidently shared by all but the French Government.[47] So long as the latter maintains its opposition, however, the meetings of the Seven, while covering a broad range of subjects,[48] will no doubt continue to be, as one high WEU official has put it, conferences where the governments "listen to each other but do not discuss."

THE EUROPEAN PARLIAMENT

Origins and Establishment

The Common Assembly of the European Coal and Steel Community came into being on September 10, 1952, and held its final meeting on March 19, 1958. It was replaced by what became the "European Parliament," which began operation on the latter date as the parliamentary organ for all three six-nation Communities — the European Coal and Steel Community (ECSC), the European Atomic Energy Community (Euratom) and the European Economic Community (EEC). The establishment of the latter two communities might well have led to the setting up of the Atlantic area's seventh international parliamentary assembly. Some of the negotiators

---

[45]Reply of the Council, April 13, 1964, ibid., p. 16.

[46]The Guardian, April 18, 1964, cited in Doc. 312, op. cit., p. 10-11.

[47]Cf. ibid., p. 9-13.

[48]E.g., GATT tariff negotiations, World Conference on Trade and Development, respective economic policies of EEC and EFTA, East-West relations, political and military consultation — cited in Recommendation 101 and accompanying reply of the Council, WEU Assembly, 10th Session, Doc. 311, June 1, 1964, p. 11-12.

of the Rome Treaties[49] reportedly felt that the provision of a less "supranational" assembly would make it easier for certain French political parties to approve ratification. The emphatic intervention of the bureaus of the Consultative, Common and WEU Assemblies ended further talk of a seventh assembly.[50] The European Parliament took over, on behalf of the three communities, the powers, functions, traditions and part of the membership of the Common Assembly.

The most important and largest part of the work of the European Parliament relates to the establishment of the Common Market. The EEC Treaty provides rules and institutions for the establishment among the signatories of a customs union and common market within a transitional period of twelve to fifteen years. The treaty took effect on January 1, 1958; the first internal tariff and quota modifications were carried out as scheduled one year later. By July 1, 1968, the common external tariffs are to be established and the internal tariffs — reduced by 80 percent as of January 1, 1966 — as well as all quota restrictions, are to be eliminated.[51]

---

[49]The Rome Treaties establishing the EEC and Euratom are published in English, with related protocols and conventions by the Secretariat of the Interim Committee for the Common Market and Euratom, Brussels. The Rome Treaties were signed on March 25, 1957, and went into effect on January 1, 1958.

[50]WEU Assembly, Rapport sur la création d'une quatrième assemblée européenne, Doc. 34, December 15, 1956; and esp. Supplementary Report, Doc. 46, April 5, 1957. Cf. A. H. Robertson, European Institutions, op. cit., p. 167–168. The decision was formalized in the Convention relating to Certain Institutions Common to the European Communities, attached to the Rome Treaties, which appears in Treaty establishing the European Economic Community and connected Documents (Publishing Services of the European Communities, 1961).

[51]European Community, Information Service, The Facts, September 1962. A useful, recent study of the European Parliament's powers and functions is Political and Economic Planning's "broadsheet," The Parliament of the European Communities (by Murray Forsyth), London: March 9, 1964 (97 pages, plus text of the Rules of Procedure). Cf. Dietrich Sperling, Der Parlamentarische Charakter Europäischer Versammlungen (Leiden: Sythoff, 1961).

By that time also, the free movement of workers is to be assured (Article 48); capital movements are to be freed "to the extent necessary for the proper functioning of the Common Market" (Article 67-1); national policies relating to transport, agriculture and external trade are to be replaced by Community policies, and some harmonization of social legislation is to be undertaken.

Internal Arrangements

To achieve these results, the EEC Treaty provides for institutions modeled broadly on those of the Coal and Steel Community. In addition to the "assembly" (which adopted the name "European Parliament" in 1962[52]) they are as follows. The Council represents the governments and determines basic policy; most of its decisions after 1965 will be — in principle at least — by qualified majority. The Commission composed of nine individuals chosen by the governments by common agreement and duty-bound to act "in the general interest of the Community with complete independence" (Article 157-2), is the executive organ of the Community. It "ensures the application" of the Treaty (Article 155), makes recommendations on all matters it deems necessary and has decision-making authority in specified instances. The Court of Justice, which the EEC shares with the Coal and Steel Community and Euratom, is authorized to act on appeals challenging the legality of acts of the Council, the Commission or member States. The Economic and Social Committee, composed of 101 individuals appointed by the Council to be representative of the various categories of economic and social life, serves as a consultative body to the Council and Commission. The European Investment Bank, with an initial capital

---

[52]The Rome Treaty uses only the word "Assembly." Until 1962 the body was known in French as the Assemblée Parlementaire Européenne. The change was adopted in 1962 ostensibly for the purpose of making the French (and Italian) designations conform to the German and Dutch. Other reasons mentioned in the debate for this decision (which had been discussed and rejected in 1958) were to avoid confusion in the public mind with the Consultative Assembly and to point up the fact that the EEC body was a "parliament in embryo."--EEC, Parlement Européen, Débats VIII/62, No. 36, 1962-63 Session, p. 136-139.

of $1 billion, provides loans and guarantees on a non-profit basis to finance projects for developing less developed regions, for modernizing or converting enterprises and for other purposes. The European Social Fund and the European Development Fund are both administered by the Commission. The former assists in the re-settling and retraining of workers, and the latter provided $581 million over the first five years of the treaty and will provide $800 million over the second five years for social and economic investment projects in the associated overseas countries and territories.

The European Parliament meets regularly seven times a year, for a total of some forty days. It can meet in extraordinary session at the request of a majority of its members or the request of the ministerial Council or the Commission (Art. 139). It usually meets at Strasbourg but has met once at Rome and once at Brussels. It exercises the "powers of deliberation and control" conferred on it by the three treaties. The unprecedented feature of those powers is the motion of censure. Article 144 of the ECC Treaty [53] provides:

> If a motion of censure concerning the activities of the Commission is introduced in the Assembly, a vote may be taken thereon only after a period of not less than three days following its introduction, and such vote shall be by open ballot.
>
> If the motion of censure is adopted by a two-thirds majority of the votes cast, representing a majority of the members of the Assembly, the members of the Commission shall resign their office in a body. They shall continue to carry out current business until their replacement in accordance with the provisions of Article 158 has taken place.

---

[53] The articles cited here and below with respect to the European Parliament are from the EEC Treaty; they are identical but differently numbered in the Euratom Treaty and are generally comparable in the ECSC Treaty, where however, censure can relate only to the High Authority's annual report. A Committee of the WEU Assembly has suggested that the right of censure should be applicable also to the Council of Ministers, but with a milder sanction, namely, that if a second revised report is likewise censured, it and the motion of censure would be referred automatically to the national parliaments, where the national minister would be required to justify his position. -- WEU Assembly, 8th Session, Future Pattern of Europe, Report of General Affairs Committee (Badini Confalonieri, Italy, Rapporteur), June 1962, p. 15.

Members of the Commission and Council may attend meetings and "shall, at their request, be heard" (Art. 140). The Parliament "shall discuss in public meeting the annual general report submitted to it by the Commission" (Art. 143) and has the right to submit questions, to which the Commission "shall reply orally or in writing" (Art. 40). A variety of provisions require that the Parliament be consulted in advance of certain decisions by the Commission or Council.

The European Parliament received a second function that is without precedent in international parliamentary bodies. Article 138-3 stipulates that the Parliament "shall draw up proposals for [its] elections by direct universal suffrage in accordance with a uniform procedure in all Member States." (The Council, however, determines what is to be recommended to the governments as well as when.) Under the plan[54] proposed by the Parliament on May 17, 1960, the popularly elected body would be enlarged as shown in Table 4. The election would take place on the same day, a Sunday, in all six countries. Representatives would serve for five years. The minimum age to vote or hold office would be 21. The Parliament proposed the establishment of a "transitional period" that would end not later than the end of the third phase in the completion of the Common Market. During the transition,

Table 4
Present and Proposed Representation
in the European Parliament

	Present (Art. 138)	Parliament's Proposal
Belgium	14	42
Germany.	36	108
France...............	36	108
Italy................	36	108
Luxembourg	6	18
Netherlands.	14	42
TOTALS...........	142	426

[54]Text in Les élections européennes au sufrage universel, Colloque des 14 et 15 avril 1960 (Editions de l'Institut de Sociologie Solvay, 1960), p. 273-282. See also Roy Price, The Political Future of the European Community (London: John Marshbank, 1962), p. 70-72 and 88-91. Also P. E. P., Direct Elections of the European Parliament, Occasional Paper No. 10, October 24, 1960.

one-third of the Assembly would be chosen by the national parliaments, and national M.P.'s could be members of the European body. The question as to compatibility thereafter between national and European parliamentary mandates would be determined by the European Parliament.

While the Parliament advocates immediate adoption of its plan, there is some feeling that the popular election of delegates would be more meaningful and perhaps more success- ful if the Parliament were first given more power and a greater role in the work of the Communities. At present it can take no decision that is binding on any of the executive policies and has no control over the finances of the Commu- nity. A variety of largely unavailing proposals to strengthen this body have been made since the inception of the Common Assembly in 1952. On June 27, 1963, the European Parlia- ment adopted a resolution of its Political Committee pro- posing:

> Parliamentary participation in the appointment of the Community Executives ....

> Consultation between the Parliament and the Council of Ministers on all important issues, even in cases where the Treaties do not specifically oblige the Council to ask for the Parliament's opinion.

> That parliamentary opinions, which are adopted by a two-thirds majority at the second reading, be binding on the Council of Ministers unless opposed by a unani- mous decision of the Council.

> Parliamentary ratification of all the Community's in- ternational agreements.

> Greater parliamentary control over the Community's finances.

> Parliamentary control of the Community's budget when the Community's expenditure is met from its own re- sources.

> Parliamentary nomination of judges for the Community's Court of Justice from lists provided by member govern- ments.[55]

---

[55]European Community, July-August 1963, No. 64, p. 7. (Informa- tion Office, European Community, Washington, D. C.) summarizing Parlement Européen, Documents de Séance, June 14, 1963, Doc. 31, Rapport sur les compétences et les pouvoirs du Parlement européen.

It is interesting that the President of the EEC Commission, Dr. Walter Hallstein, shares the view that the Parliament's powers should be increased. He told the Parliament in October 1962, for example, "The European Parliament's position must be strengthened by means of direct elections and by increasing its share in Community legislation and its powers of supervision.... We regard the strengthening of Parliament's role as the most essential point of constitutional progress."[56] In 1965, the Commission proposed measures to strengthen the Parliament's role in determining the Community's budget.

In accordance with an early decision of the Common Assembly, the members of the Parliament sit by Community-wide party groupings rather than by national groups as in the NPC or individually as in the Consultative Assembly. The four political groups — the Christian Democrats, the Liberals, the Socialists and the Gaullistes — usually formulate their views in advance of debates, and the votes are generally on party lines. (There has been a similar development in the Consultative and WEU Assemblies, and in the latter, as in the Parliament, funds are provided for party group meetings.)

There are 13 standing committees: Political Affairs, External Trade, Agriculture, Social Affairs, Internal Market, Economic and Financial Affairs, Relations with Underdeveloped Countries, Transport, Energy, Research and Cultural Affairs, Health Protection, Administration and Budget, Legal Affairs.[57] Every member is on one or more committees, which can meet at any time. The principal documents of the Parliament are the Journal Officiel and the Annuaire-Manuel.

Practice and Program

Each edition of the Annuaire-Manuel of the European Parliament contains scores of reports and dozens of resolutions and detailed opinions. The Assembly has had important debates on political questions, such as those in which most members expressed bitter reactions to the French veto

---

[56] European Community, ibid., p. 8. On April 8, 1965, the Foreign Ministers of the Six signed the Traité instituant un Conseil unique et une Commission unique des Communautés Européennes. The treaty, now in the process of ratification, would merge the three executives into a single Commission comprising fourteen persons during the first three years and nine thereafter.

[57] Parlement Européen, Reglement, Arts. 37–43.

of Britain's application for membership in the EEC and those concerning the recent seven-month crisis precipitated by the French boycott of Community institutions. Most of the deliberations, however, are of a far more technical nature, dealing (by way of illustration out of recent meetings) with such matters as "criteria for fixing target prices for farm produce," "freedom of establishment" with respect to wholesale trade, the operational accounts and balance sheets of the EEC and Euratom Commissions, an "action program for the common transport policy," and "freedom to supply services." In these debates, members of the Executives usually take an active part.

The European Parliament has powers never before given to an international parliamentary assembly, yet it remains essentially consultative. The nature of its work requires a far more elaborate structure and system of rules and, in proportion to the number of member countries, a substantially larger budget. The most significant innovations of this institution are its right to censure the executive commissions with the effect of compelling their resignation and its statutory prospect of being elected by direct, universal suffrage. These and the other attributes that distinguish the European Parliament from the other European assemblies are traceable primarily to the fact that the member states have assigned "limited but real" powers to the executives, whose vast and complex tasks, it was recognized, required a form of parliamentary supervision that could not be assured without an assembly internationally constituted and liberally endowed with funds and staff.

CONCLUSIONS

The prestige of the Consultative Assembly of the Council of Europe has undoubtedly declined in recent years. Some of its glamour has been pre-empted by the European Parliament since the early days when the debates in Strasbourg were sparked by such men as Churchill, Reynaud, Schuman and Spaak. Yet the Assembly continues to play a constructive role in European politics. Its debates have helped clarify important international issues and have sharpened public interest in the problems and prospects of European unification. Its studies and recommendations have led to the adoption of a wide range of international conventions for closer technical and cultural cooperation. Its example has promoted the establishment of five other interparliamentary bodies. Its failures as well as its successes have provided the experience out of which parliamentarians could devise significant improvements in the methods and procedures of interparliamentary consultation. The Consultative Assembly, in short, pioneered a concept and a technique that have served Europe well in the postwar years and that, properly adapted, might now find their most valuable application in the context of Atlantic cooperation.

The Assembly of Western European Union, despite its self-designed charter and procedure — both of which merit careful study by those interested in an Atlantic Assembly — has had a less happy experience with international consultation. It might well be that in any major reorganization of the assemblies, that of WEU would be the first to disappear. WEU's economic and social functions have been transferred in toto to the Council of Europe. The Assembly's performance as the watchdog of European defense, while generally acknowledged as useful and unique, has been handicapped by the fact that European defense is organized through the North Atlantic Alliance, eight of whose member-states, including the United States, are outside WEU. The current effort of the Assembly to make WEU the main vehicle of rapprochement between the Six and Britain is not likely to prove productive so long as France maintains its present position on the principle of British participation in the European Communities, and there is no evidence that the discussions in the WEU Council are likely to affect that position significantly. With regard to the Assembly's role in overseeing WEU's arms control activities — the main justification originally given for establishment of the Assembly — it has long been clear that the problem in Europe is not the limitation of armaments but their increase to agreed levels. Most of the arms control activity in any event is too technical and specialized to require close parliamentary scrutiny. Ironically, the most important recommendations that the Assembly has had occasion to submit to the Council in this field have been largely disregarded by the seven governments.

The unsatisfactory experience of the WEU Assembly supports the view that effective consultation between an assembly and an executive agency depends in part upon a clear definition of their respective competences and mutual responsibilities. The anomalies in the position of the WEU Assembly, considered in conjunction with other developments, have led the Assembly to contemplate its own dissolution or its merger with another body. There is little question that parliamentary discussion of Western defense could best take place in a body whose membership coincides with or includes that of the North Atlantic Alliance as a whole, and there would seem to be no reason of principle why the other functions of the WEU Assembly could not be performed, for example, by restricted committees of a consultative Atlantic Assembly. Thus far, however, for reasons to be considered below, the WEU Assembly has entertained the idea of merging only with a European Parliament enlarged by the admission of Britain and perhaps other EFTA nations into the European Communities.

The organizers of the WEU Assembly were influenced not only by their experience in the Consultative Assembly but also by the example of the Common Assembly, predecessor of the European Parliament. The Parliament enjoys powers and facilities that, in important respects, will remain inapplicable to the Atlantic Community until such time as the latter may decide to establish executive institutions of comparable "supranationality."

5

The dilemma, and the opportunity, of a consultative assembly lies in the fact that the execution of its wishes depends entirely upon the interest and capacity of the governments and the executive agencies to respond. The problem of promoting that interest and capacity is complicated by the fact that the assembly's resolutions do not engage the responsibility of the individuals and political parties initiating and voting them.

Consultative parliamentary bodies, including the NATO Parliamentarians' Conference, have frequently heard but less often heeded suggestions from their members to support the recommendations in their national parliaments and constituencies. The absence of an effective obligation to do so has had two undesirable consequences. It has encouraged the adoption of impracticable "operative" resolutions, and it has impeded the transfer of valid proposals to the only arena where they can be implemented.

The ability of an assembly to obtain a wider and more attentive hearing for a resolution depends on three factors — the timeliness and concreteness of the resolution, the assembly's relationship with the executive agency, and the procedures that may be adopted for following up and exerting pressure at the national level.

The third of these factors — follow-up in the national parliaments and ministries — has potentialities that parliamentarians have increasingly recognized in recent years. Since 1956, the Consultative Assembly has developed a technique that appears to have considerably widened the impact of its resolutions, and it is a technique that could prove of comparable value to the NATO Parliamentarians' Conference or an eventual Atlantic Assembly. As will be suggested, there are perhaps additional steps that consultative assemblies might take to perfect their follow-up procedures.

THE NATO PARLIAMENTARIANS' CONFERENCE

The problem of implementation has come in for sporadic attention in the debates of the NATO Parliamentarians'

Conference and was particularly well defined by Lord Ogmore in the Seventh Session:

> I have been coming here for the last five years and I have never heard what has happened to any of our resolutions, except some of those which become apparent because we have seen them come to fruition, such as the Atlantic Institute, the Citizen's Congress, and to some extent I think also the OECD. Apart from those, the many resolutions that have come forward have so far as we are concerned vanished into space, and it is desirable, in the opinion of the Political Committee, that every year we should know from the North Atlantic Council what has happened to the children which we have laid on their doorstep.[1]

Senator Javits touched on this problem in the Eighth Session as follows:

> It is one thing to come here and make our speeches, to adopt our Resolutions, to do our hard work and to develop our ideas, but it is another thing to go back and see that these are implemented in our own legislatures. I am proud to say that, for myself, and for a number of other members of the American Delegation, time and again we have arisen in our respective bodies... and have contended for propositions in line with the actions taken by the NATO Parliamentarians, invoking the NATO Parliamentarians as authority. We have made reports to our respective bodies of the work which has taken place. ... [2]

At the same session, Dr. Fritz Burgbacher (Federal Republic of Germany) urged the Conference to decide "(a) that the Delegations should, in their yearly reports, inform the Conference of what has happened in connection with the various resolutions, and what measures have been taken in the member countries; (b) that the rapporteurs of the Commissions should also report on the progress which has been made by NATO and/or the difficulties in fulfilling the resolutions."[3]

---

[1]NPC, Verbatim Report, 7th Session, November 16, a.m., 1961, p. 38.

[2]Ibid., 6th Session, November 25, p.m., 1960, p. 88.

[3]Ibid., p. 55.

A step in the direction of closer checks on implementation was adopted by the Cultural Affairs and Information Committee and announced in the Eighth Session by Senator Carl Mundt. The Committee had named a second rapporteur with a view to having four committee officers "available to monitor the recommendations which we have made, to measure the progress, to study the results of this annual survey of what each country is doing individually and what remains to be done by NATO."[4] The move was, as he acknowledged, analogous to the Working Party arrangement adopted earlier by the Economic Committee.[5] A further step in the same direction was the decision in the Ninth Session to appoint a General Rapporteur.[6]

The problem of implementation has been more thoroughly explored in the Consultative Assembly of the Council of Europe. The terms and fate of its efforts to date should be instructive for the NATO Parliamentarians' Conference.

THE CONSULTATIVE ASSEMBLY—METHODS AND RESULTS

The Consultative Assembly of the Council of Europe was, for the historical reasons already indicated, endowed from the beginning with a governmental organ, the Committee of Ministers. The existence of this body has tended to confuse and embitter the work of the Council's Consultative Assembly without adding anything real to the means by which the decision-making authority of the member governments was protected against undue interference from "irresponsible" parliamentary consultation. The Consultative Assembly's attack on the problem of implementation began modestly. It began, as Fernand Dehousse's comprehensive memorandum of 1956 to the Assembly recalls, with a recommendation adopted in the Second Session "that the Committee of

---

[4]Ibid., 8th Session, November 16, a.m., 1962, p. 42.

[5]Senator Javits had proposed the appointment of a seven-member Working Party or subcommittee of the Economic Committee to work with him and the President of the Conference to implement the resolution on investment in Latin America. --Ibid., p. 33 and ibid., p.m., p. 67.

[6]See above, Conclusions, Chapter 2.

Ministers, by majority of its members, invite Governments to submit to their parliaments such recommendations or draft conventions as the Assembly may recommend...."[7]

In its subsequent frustration, according to the Dehousse memorandum, the Assembly decided that

> resolutions selected by the Standing Committee from among those passed by the Assembly should be "communicated to the Governments of all Member States of the Council of Europe and to all Members of Parliaments of these States." The Representatives to the Assembly undertook "to do their utmost to secure that such resolutions, selected by the Standing Committee, shall as quickly as possible be presented to their respective parliaments for discussion." Representatives who had voted for these resolutions undertook "to use their best endeavours" to ensure their adoption by their respective parliaments. [8]

These proposals, as Dehousse candidly observed, "came to nothing."[9] In the Seventh Session (1955), the Consultative Assembly therefore adopted a further resolution. Considering that "systematic relations should be established between the Consultative Assembly and the national Parliaments," the Assembly:

A. Invites the Representatives from each Member

> 1. to do their utmost — by setting up a Special Committee for questions concerning the Council of Europe, by intervention in general debates, by tabling a written question, by giving notice of an oral question or interpellation, by introduction of a bill, etc. — to bring about, whenever appropriate, a discussion in their respective Parliaments of recommendations made by the Consultative Assembly which call on the Committee of Ministers or the

---

[7]Recommendation 14 (1950), cited in Council of Europe, Consultative Assembly, 8th Session, Report on Relations between the Consultative Assembly and National Parliaments, Doc. 529, September 8, 1956, p. 3. Document 529 is cited hereinafter as Dehousse Memorandum.

[8]Dehousse Memorandum, ibid., p. 3.

[9]Ibid.

national Parliaments to take a decision on a particular question;

2. to arrange for texts adopted by the Consultative Assembly on a given question to be brought to the attention of Parliament whenever there is any discussion of the same question;

3. to present to Parliament a report on the work of the Consultative Assembly after each Session or part-Session;

4. to make the necessary arrangements to ensure that action on these lines is taken in good time; to this end, Representatives from each member country might appoint one or more Representatives who, assisted by a permanent administrative secretary, and in cooperation with the Clerk of the Assembly, would be responsible for the implementation of the measures suggested above;

B. Invites the President of the Consultative Assembly to send to national Parliaments, with appropriate comments, those of the texts adopted by the Assembly which, in the opinion of the Bureau, it would be of particular value to bring to the attention of members of national Parliaments;

C. Instructs the Clerk of the Assembly to take all necessary steps towards the implementation of this Resolution, and, in particular, to provide Representatives with:

(a) the texts which are to be sent to national Parliaments in accordance with Section A, paragraphs 1 and 2;

(b) the information necessary for the preparation of the reports referred to in Section A, paragraph 3.[10]

Within a year after the adoption of that resolution, the Assembly had concluded that a procedure relying essentially

---

[10] Council of Europe, Consultative Assembly, Texts Adopted, 7th Session, July 7, 1955, Resolution 70.

the voluntary and unorganized efforts of its participants for implementation at the national level was insufficient. This conclusion followed the argument of the Dehousse Memorandum, which observed that informing the national parliaments of the Assembly's work and getting them to take it up in a timely and adequate manner posed four practical problems: the selection of the appropriate resolutions; their translation; their printing and distribution; and their introduction into the parliamentary process.

The ensuing resolution took another logical step, and the most successful to date, in organizing better response to Assembly recommendations. It established a standing committee — the Working Party — with a mandate to promote, report on, and evaluate action at the national level. The resolution[11] provided for the systematic selection, translation, printing, and distribution of Assembly recommendations and for the organization of the Working Party responsible to make the necessary arrangements, to report periodically on

---

[11]The text was as follows:

1. There shall be set up a permanent working party with the general task of maintaining close links between the Consultative Assembly and national parliaments.
2. This Working Party shall be made up of seven members freely appointed by the Bureau. It shall elect a Chairman. It shall meet as often as it considers appropriate.
3. The Working Party shall select texts from among those adopted by the Consultative Assembly for transmission to the national parliaments. Where necessary, it shall decide what funds are required for the translation, printing and distribution of the selected texts.
4. It shall provide the Assembly each year with a general picture of the action taken in the national parliaments to implement the Assembly's decisions.
5. After each Session of the Assembly, it shall assist the national delegations or their individual members in whatever steps they undertake to present the results of the Assembly's work to their own parliaments.
6. The Working Party shall, accordingly, establish all the necessary contacts, in particular with the Chairmen of the political groups, the Committee Chairmen and Rapporteurs, the spokesmen and the secretaries of the national delegations.
7. As soon as the Working Party deems it appropriate, it should report to the Assembly on how far the methods laid down in the present Resolution are proving effective for their purpose, and submit whatever further proposals are called for. --Ibid., 8th Session, October 25, 1956, Resolution 104.

the results, and to propose, as experience might dictate, improvements in the procedure as adopted.

In approving that resolution, the Assembly had accepted the essentials of a draft embodied in the Dehousse Memorandum. On the other hand, it had rejected two Dehousse proposals that had envisaged a more elaborate apparatus. One would have required the national delegation to appoint "whips" responsible for organizing the follow-up at the national level. In the resolution as adopted this borrowed notion of the "whip" was reduced to "spokesman" and might better have been reduced further, as Paul Struye (Belgium) suggested, to "correspondent."[12]

The other issue was considerably less a matter of terminology. The Dehousse draft resolution had proposed that each national delegation establish a full-time, professional position of "parliamentary attaché" to replace the national civil servants who were customarily detached from "unrelated" parliamentary or foreign office duties to assist the delegations during the periods of Assembly sessions. In Dehousse's conception, the parliamentary attachés "would translate the relevant texts and would give them a suitable form for presentation to the parliament of their country. They would draw up reports on the work of the Sessions of the Consultative Assembly for submission to their parliaments and would help the whips prepare for the Working Party a progress report on the work of the national delegations in their parliaments."

The debate on that idea indicated that most delegations did not believe the additional advantages would outweigh the additional cost. Consequently, as Karl Mommer (Federal Republic of Germany, the Rapporteur) explained, the Bureau had lowered its sights and was merely urging delegations "to make the fullest possible use of their available secretarial facilities."[13] The final resolution was adopted, 69 to 0 with 4 abstentions, on October 25, 1956. The few reservations expressed indicated doubts that even if the Working Party could in practice be convened outside of Assembly sessions it was unlikely to serve any real function not already carried

---

[12]Ibid., Official Report of Debates, 8th Session, October 25, 1956, p. 838.

[13]Ibid.

out by the delegations themselves and the Secretariat. To these caveats the Bureau's rapporteur replied in effect that the Working Party would need to meet only during sessions, that only parliamentarians could effectively press parliamentarians for the desired action, and that less formal procedures had been tried in the past without noticeable success.

In summary, the Working Party thus established was designed to promote fuller implementation of selected Assembly recommendations by encouraging and assisting the efforts of Representatives to obtain appropriate discussion and action in their national parliaments. The manner in which this experiment has evolved over the ensuing seven years merits close examination in connection with any reorganization of Atlantic parliamentary consultation.

The Working Party has held an average of seven meetings a year, generally during the Assembly's tripartite sessions, and since 1959 has also met at least once a year in the capital of a Member. The seven-man body was enlarged in 1957 to include one participant (and one alternate) per country. The participation of alternates permits representation of two political parties per country. This has the twin advantage of increasing the points of contact in the national parliament and of improving the chances that a given Assembly recommendation will be pressed upon the national government.[14] The principal components of the system are the Working Party member (who is usually at the same time the spokesman of the national delegation), the secretary of the national delegation (usually on temporary assignment from the staff of the national parliament or, in some instances, of the Foreign Ministry), and the Working Party secretary and staff (drawn from the Council of Europe's Secretariat). Operation of this system to date has led the Working Party to recommend that each delegation designate one spokesman per political group represented;[15] and that delegation staffs be enabled through increase in size or exemption from other duties, to give more time to Assembly affairs.[16]

---

[14]Cf. A. Glenn Mower, Jr., "The Official Pressure Group of the Council of Europe's Consultative Assembly," International Organization, Vol. XVIII, No. 2 (Boston: World Peace Foundation, Spring 1964), p. 292-306.

[15]Council of Europe, Consultative Assembly, Fourth Annual Report of the Working Party, Doc. 1193, September 19, 1960, p. 6.

[16]Ibid., Fifth Annual Report of the Working Party, Doc. 1306, July 1, 1961, p. 5.

In selecting the Assembly texts to be translated, distributed and promoted at the national level, the Working Party has sought to apply the criteria of concreteness, precision and relevance to the major concerns of member countries.[17] The proportion of texts selected in a given session has ranged from over 70 percent (1960-1961) to about 33 percent (1962-1963).[18] In addition, the Working Party regularly reexamines previously selected texts and chooses some of these for renewed effort.

The Working Party not only selects the texts to be pressed at the national level, but suggests the kind of pressure that is likely to prove most fruitful. Such pressure may take the form of presenting a report, raising a parliamentary question, or introducing a resolution in the national legislature, holding a private interview with the appropriate minister or other official, making a speech in parliament, initiating a debate, or proposing the inclusion of designated material in a committee report.[19]

Undertaking to recommend tactics as well as texts has led the Working Party to prepare a manual on the parliamentary procedures of member countries and a summary of the tactical possibilities offered by the various parliamentary systems.[20] For the same purpose the Working Party has

---

[17]This has led the group to urge that the Assembly be prepared to adopt a resolution by a smaller majority rather than watering it down in the search for the widest possible consensus.

[18]The following tabulation is given in Mower, op. cit., p. 299:

Year	Total Consultative Assembly Texts Available	Texts Chosen	Previous Texts Reexamined	Previous Texts Reselected
1956-57	80	45		
1957-58	48	24	45	18
1958-59	59	33	62	29
1959-60	56	38	86	24
1960-61	56	41	90	24
1961-62	65	22	74	17
1962-63	74	26	49	10

[19]Council of Europe, Consultative Assembly, Doc. 640, Appendix 4, April 26, 1957.

[20]Ibid., Fourth Annual Report of the Working Party, Doc. 1193, September 19, 1960, p. 12 ff.

arranged to receive the regular agendas of a number of the parliaments. Finally, the Working Party further assists the delegation spokesmen by providing background memoranda on the texts and by suggesting drafts of appropriate parliamentary questions.

The immediate results of this operation are reported in a series of Working Party circulars issued periodically (usually one for each of the three parts of each session) under the title, "Activity of National Parliaments on Council of Europe Affairs." Twenty-one French-English circulars, varying in length from some 40 to 200 pages each, were published between 1957 and July 1963. The information is presented by country under three headings: documents tabled (draft resolutions, motions, questions, etc.); proceedings devoted wholly or in part to Council of Europe affairs (debates, announcements, oral questions); and individual steps by parliamentarians to ministers or other persons. Dated entries under each heading may provide summary or verbatim extracts of the pertinent national documents. The series constitutes a highly informative and comprehensive running catalogue of the more important activities of the Assembly, of the follow-up arranged by Assembly participants, and, to the extent indicated in debate or replies, of the policies followed or contemplated in respect of such matters by the national governments. The emergence of this new publication, Strasbourg officials feel, has itself served as a further stimulus to the promotional effort, by providing a highly selective outlet for individual interventions as well as a basis for friendly rivalry among delegations.

Countries not reporting in the period covered by a circular are listed with the notation "no report." In the first six sessions for which complete data are available, only one country (Iceland) has consistently failed to file information (reporting only and perfunctorily in the 11th session). During that period, apart from the first year of the experiment (when four countries went unreported), only one or two countries per session have failed to report.

In short, most national delegations report regularly and their reports, detailed and comprehensive, reveal that they have frequently resorted to the full range of suggested follow-up methods. It is clearly no longer possible to charge, as participants frequently did prior to 1957, that Assembly resolutions are ignored by the national parliaments and governments. It is apparent that the effort has increased the activity within the parliaments, not merely the assembly's awareness of such activity. The immediate objective of the Working Party operation has thus been achieved.[21]

The ultimate objective is of course to induce compliance – for example the ratification of a draft convention, the modification of domestic legislation, or the adoption of a particular policy – on the part of the national governments. It is clear, and hardly surprising, that this objective has been achieved to a much lesser extent. As the circulars confirm, governments frequently reject Assembly proposals, often for the most plausible reasons; much more often they evade or ignore the questions that the Working Party operation has placed before them. It is, moreover, seldom possible, with any certainty, to attribute a positive official position to the fact that an Assembly representative has raised a question, filed a motion, or initiated a debate. A government policy is the resultant of many forces, and, in general, the best that can be said for the Working Party is that its effort in a particular instance may have been among the contributing factors.

The Working Party has rightly pointed with satisfaction to the fact that, "following parliamentary questions suggested by the Working Party, individual governments expressed more and more their attitudes towards the recommendations of the Assembly. In doing so they gave the Assembly valuable information which the Committee of Ministers, in virtue of

---

[21]According to a tabulation by Mower (op. cit., p. 304), the results have been as follows:

Year	Documents Tabled (Motions, Questions, Draft Bills)	Special or General Debates	Individual Approaches to Ministers	Total
1956–57	89	18	12	119
1957–58	119	54	32	205
1958–59	151	124	41	316
1959–60	167	110	32	309
1960–61 (10 months)	174	82	28	284
1961–62	194	99	27	320
1962–63	220	104	26	350

their rules of procedure, cannot reveal."[22] The Working Party's further claim, however, that its efforts "have assisted in getting governments to adopt, in many cases, a favorable attitude" is, as noted, plausible but less readily demonstrable.

The partial but impressive results of this follow-up program led the Consultative Assembly to conclude that the Working Party's reach should be extended and its techniques applied to public as well as to parliamentary relations. In May 1963 the Assembly accordingly voted to broaden the Working Party's terms of reference, and preparations followed for a new kind of Strasbourg campaign, aimed primarily at the press.

Another and far more radical suggestion designed to improve implementation was advanced as early as May 1, 1957, by the then President of the WEU Assembly. Under that proposal, regional assembly recommendations would receive the approval of the national parliament by means of automatic referral and a procedure analogous to that of a "negative resolution." Referring to the practice in the United Kingdom, the President of the Assembly said:

> We have in our country a system whereby certain actions taken by the Government automatically become law unless they are opposed by Parliament. It is known as the system of the Negative Resolution; I wonder whether we cannot evolve a system whereby, with a smaller agenda and with more expert advice available to us, after we have deeply thought out some of our problems and have put forward resolutions to our national Governments, those resolutions would automatically have the force of law unless they are opposed in our Parliaments? ... If ... those Parliaments in fact approved those resolutions, they then would become an instruction from the combination of Parliaments to the Council of Ministers, who at that stage, should be the Council of Prime Ministers, and the resolutions would then have all the force of law. This of course would imply that our resolutions would have to be considered with extreme care and with all the sense of responsibility that legislators would then have....[23]

---

[22]Fifth Annual Report of the Working Party, Doc. 1306, July 1, 1961, op. cit., p. 9.

[23]Sir James Hutchinson, quoted in WEU Assembly, 3d Session, The Unification of European Assemblies, Report of General Affairs Committee (J. M. van der Goes van Naters, Rapporteur), Doc. 62, September 21, 1957, p. 5 and 13-14. Cf. proposals of Italian Government, submitted

CONCLUSIONS

The ability of individual parliamentarians to exercise influence on government policy depends not only upon their personal prestige and party responsibilities, but also upon other factors, such as the relative strengths of the parties in parliament and the constitutional modes by which policies are proposed, adopted and implemented. Since the effect of consultative assembly resolutions must depend in part upon the follow-up efforts of the members when they return home, the caliber of the participants is doubly important. Selection of participants in the NATO Parliamentarians' Conference has tended to assure representation of the main non-Communist parties and to reflect a range of views on Atlantic affairs that is not limited to enthusiasts of Atlantic integration. This is one of the strengths of the Conference from the standpoint of implementation of resolutions.

The experience of that body and even more so of the Consultative Assembly, however, has demonstrated that reliance on purely voluntary and unorganized efforts of the individual parliamentarians produces spotty results at best. That Conference participants have reached similar conclusions is indicated by their decision to establish committee Working Parties and a new position of General Rapporteur.

The work of Dehousse and the Bureau of the Consultative Assembly starting in 1955 served to identify more clearly than theretofore some of the other tasks an assembly must perform if it is to exert its maximal impact on national and regional policy. The appropriate resolutions must be selected. They must be translated from the two official languages into, in that body, nine others — German, Italian, Dutch, Danish, Norwegian, Icelandic, Greek, Portuguese and Turkish. They must be distributed. Their substance must then be introduced into the legislative and governmental processes. To facilitate that effort, background memoranda and appropriate parliamentary questions or motions must be drafted to accompany the selected resolutions. Reports from the national delegations on the results of such activity must be requested, assembled, collated, analyzed, published and distributed. The whole procedure must be reviewed and revised in the light of further experience.

---

by Martino to Western European Union Council of Ministers on December 10, 1956 (Doc. A/WEU/B (57) 8). (Explained to Consultative Assembly on May 3, 1957).

The Consultative Assembly has found that this requires, in addition to intensive staff work, the establishment of a standing committee of representatives qualified to act as delegation spokesmen and prepared to devote considerable time to the task. Given those conditions, the procedure has proven effective. In the case of the Consultative Assembly, it has greatly increased the number of parliamentary démarches in the national capitals and led to many more debates, motions and questions and answers than had been the case previously. How far those results in turn may have modified the policies or hastened the actions of the governments is a question that, for lack of pertinent evidence, must remain speculative.

Whether the NATO Parliamentarians' Conference could adopt this procedure would depend perhaps primarily on the availability of additional funds. Meanwhile, it may be suggested, an alternative, if not a supplement, to that procedure might well be found in the development of a technique by which, with respect to selected "operative" resolutions, a vote in favor entails a personal obligation to take or endorse certain specific actions at home.

The follow-up possibilities open to individual participants will vary widely, but they could range from the presentation of a bill in the national legislature or a proposal in a party caucus, to the initiation of a parliamentary question, a press conference or a public speech. The precise definition of the minimum common obligation might be incorporated in the resolution, which might also enumerate other measures that could be taken voluntarily to the same purpose. Whatever the action, it would be designed to give specific and maximum support nationally to the details of the resolution to which the obligation applies.

This "parliamentary compact," as it might be called, would apply only to resolutions that specifically invoke the procedure and that obtain whatever qualified majority may be stipulated in the rules for important questions. The actions taken by the individuals or, as the case may be, by the party groups or national delegations collectively, would be the subject of a mandatory report at the next session of the Conference.

The result, it may be anticipated, might be a somewhat smaller number of resolutions per session, and a distinct increase in the public and governmental consideration that is the prerequisite to responsive action.

Consultative assemblies are without power, but not without influence. The measures considered here can enhance their influence and to that extent perhaps contribute to what Christian Herter, among others, has suggested could be their natural evolution toward higher forms of parliamentary responsibility.[24]

---

[24]Christian A. Herter, "Atlantica," Foreign Affairs, Vol. 41, No. 2, January 1963, p. 306-308.

CHAPTER 6 RATIONALIZING INTERPARLIAMENTARY CONSULTATION— EARLY EFFORTS

There are, as has been noted in Chapter 1, six international parliamentary consultative assemblies in the West, and in varying degrees they overlap in purpose, powers, method and membership. The establishment of the OECD has inspired proposals for a seventh. The situation has generated much interest but little progress to date in "rationalization," that is, in a realignment of function among the existing institutions and a reduction of their number. The aims of most proposals for rationalization in this sense are, first, to eliminate duplication of work and economize the time and funds of participants; second, to put the regional executive and parliamentary institutions into a more effective inter-relationship; and third, to reduce confusion in public opinion. The NATO Parliamentarians' Conference has gone on record as believing that the West needs only two international parliamentary assemblies — one for the Atlantic "partnership" and the other for European integration.

Of the six existing bodies, the Benelux Consultative Parliamentary Council with its 3 members and 49 delegates, like the Nordic Council with its 4 members and 53 delegates, is sufficiently specialized in function and restricted in membership to assure virtual immunity from rationalization schemes. Rationalization will involve mainly or solely the European Parliament, the Assembly of Western European Union, the Consultative Assembly of the Council of Europe and the NATO Parliamentarians' Conference.

In advocating in 1962 an evolution toward two assemblies, the NPC Political Committee evidently had in mind that reasonably foreseeable events would permit an amalgamation of the European Parliament and the Consultative Assembly, and that a reorganized NATO Parliamentarians' Conference could readily take over the remaining functions of the WEU Assembly. This prospect, like many others, was altered by General de Gaulle's press conference of January 14, 1963. Until Great Britain and other EFTA nations are admitted to the European Community, there can be no serious question of merging its assembly with that of the Council of Europe.

108

As will be suggested below, however, there would appear to be no important reason of policy to impede a merger in some form of the NPC and the Assembly of WEU. A case can also be made, though it is more liable to challenge, that the functions of the Consultative Assembly could now be transferred to a reorganized trans-Atlantic parliamentary body.

CRITERIA

Theoretically, the most satisfactory rationalization of European-Atlantic parliamentary institutions would undertake: to assure complete correlation between functions and participants; to reduce to a minimum the number of institutions required for that purpose; to maximize the opportunity for contacts and joint activity among the representatives of all nations of the Atlantic community; to meet the special requirements of the European neutrals; to impose no inhibition on the parliamentary consultative process in the sphere of regional defense. The present chapter will examine the principal early proposals for rationalizing interparliamentary consultation. Current proposals will be considered in Chapter 7. An attempt will then be made to suggest an "optimum" theoretical rationalization. The assumptions of that scheme will form the basis for the profile or model of a consultative Atlantic Assembly proposed in Chapter 8.

THE EDEN PLAN AND RELATIONS BETWEEN "THE SIX" AND THE COUNCIL OF EUROPE

The first major attempt at what might be termed a rationalization of European parliamentary institutions was the Eden Plan, which the British Government proposed to the Committee of Ministers of the Council of Europe in March 1952. It contemplated in essence a remodelling of the Council of Europe so that it could provide the ministerial and parliamentary institutions of the European Coal and Steel Community, the European Defense Community and any other "restricted communities" that might be created. A British Aide-Memoire of that month suggested that for that purpose "a satisfactory 'two tier' system could be evolved which would enable the Council of Europe to continue its work as an organisation for intergovernmental cooperation in Western Europe. On occasion, the Committee of Ministers and the Assembly could meet on a 6-power basis to transact business connected with the Coal and Steel Community, the Defence Community, and any future organisations of the same type and membership."[1] At the tenth session of the Committee of Ministers on May 19, Eden listed five advantages of his proposal: the Council of Europe would become an integral part of the European Community; the Council would be given valuable work to do; duplication of effort would be avoided; the restricted communities would be provided with ready-made machinery; an appropriate form of association would be established between Britain (and other countries) and the European Community.

The Committee of Ministers approved the Eden Plan in principle and transmitted it to the Consultative Assembly for an opinion on the means of implementation. The British soon found it necessary to answer charges that the proposal represented an attempt to acquire power without responsibility and to exert a dampening influence on a movement that the British were presumed to oppose. There was the further apprehension that in such a structure, as a Belgian newspaper commented, "the purely consultative voice of a powerful Great Britain [would] carry greater weight than the deliberative voice of the weak Grand Duchy or even of Belgium."[2] Eden's denial, in his speech to the Assembly on September 15, 1952, threw more light on what was at best a vague proposal: the recommendations, he said,

> do not lay down detailed machinery, nor do they dictate constitutional doctrine. Their purpose is to link the communities with the rest of Western Europe without impairing their independence. There is no intention of subordinating them to the Council of Europe, still less to make the Council of Europe a court of appeal against them. They would retain their full independence; to develop freely, and to exercise the powers and functions which have been conferred on them by the six nations.... None of us who are not members of the

---

[1]The full text of the British proposal appears in Council of Europe, op. cit., Documents, 1952, Doc. 11. The Eden Plan is mentioned above in Chapter 4 in connection with the role of the Council of Europe in European integration.

[2]La Cîté, Brussels, cited in "The Council of Europe, Consultative Assembly, a Report on the Fourth Session, Part I" by the present writer (American Committee on United Europe, 1952), p. 15.

six could expect to have the right to attend their meetings unless invited to do so. But I would hope that the link with the Council of Europe which I have proposed, would make it easy and natural for the communities to share a great deal of their thought with the rest of us.

Our object was to suggest the means and promote the action, by which the two main trends toward European unity, the supranational and the intergovernmental, could be linked together. . . .[3]

In the previous May the Assembly had approved "the general principle" of the Eden Plan with the caveat that its implementation should not be allowed to "hamper in any way" the unification of the Six.[4] In September the Assembly unanimously adopted a proposal looking toward an implementation of the Plan through the following measures: (1) the non-Six Members of the Council of Europe should be invited to establish permanent delegations to the High Authority of the Coal and Steel Community; (2) the Six should permanently maintain the seat of the Common Assembly at the seat of the Council of Europe and utilize the latter's buildings and secretariat; (3) the same Representatives should, as far as possible, be appointed to both assemblies; (4) representatives to the Consultative Assembly from countries not members of the ECSC should be permitted, through agreement between the two assemblies, to take part in the proceedings of the Common Assembly and have the right to speak but not to vote; (5) the proceedings of the two assemblies on matters of mutual interest should be closely coordinated; (6) the Committee of Ministers should seek observer status in the ECSC Council of Ministers; (7) the Committee of Ministers should adopt a protocol to the Statute authorizing itself and the Consultative Assembly to serve as the ministerial and parliamentary organs of any European Community whose aims were within the scope of the Statute. [5]

Some but not all of those recommendations have been carried out. A "Protocol on Relations with the Council of

---

[3]Council of Europe, Consultative Assembly, 4th Session, Official Report of Debates, September 15, 1952, p. 281-282.

[4]Ibid., Texts Adopted, 4th Session, May 30, 1952, Resolution II.

[5]Ibid., September 30, 1952, Opinion 3.

Europe" was added to the ECSC Treaty on April 18, 1951, providing: (1) that the member governments "are invited to recommend to their respective parliaments" that the partici- pants in the Common Assembly be chosen from among the Representatives to the Consultative Assembly; (2) that the Common Assembly shall forward annually to the Consultative Assembly a report on its activity; (3) that the ECSC High Authority will communicate each year to the Committee of Ministers the annual report it prepares for the Common Assembly; (4) that the High Authority will inform the Council of Europe of "the action which it has been able to take" on any recommendations it receives from the Committee of Ministers; (5) that the ECSC Treaty and its annexes will be registered with the Secretariat of the Council of Europe; (6) that agreements between the Community and the Council of Europe may provide for other forms of mutual assistance and collaboration.[6] In addition, under the "Monnet–Layton Plan," joint sessions of the two assemblies have been held annually since June 1953. Members of the Community executives have attended meetings of committees of the Consultative Assembly, and there have been joint meetings of the Community execu- tives and the Committee of Ministers. Finally, as noted in Chapter 4, the European Parliament has úsually met at the seat of the Council of Europe, although it no longer utilizes any of the services of the latter's Secretariat.

The proposal that Consultative Assembly Representatives from the Six should be appointed to what is now the European Parliament was only partly implemented at the outset, and today for practical reasons of workload no representative of the one takes part in the other. As previously noted in con- nection with relations between the WEU and Consultative Assemblies, identity of membership (in French, union per- sonnelle) was conceived, somewhat optimistically, as a means of preventing duplication of activity among groups having overlapping competences. The WEU Assembly's General Af- fairs Committee, while favoring "some identity of member- ship" between those two bodies, has pointed out that this will be "virtually impossible" unless the European Parliament agrees to the introduction of alternate representatives.[7] These

[6]Text of protocol in European Yearbook, Vol. I (The Hague: Martinus Nijhoff, 1955), p. 451–453.

[7]WEU Assembly, Proceedings, 4th Session, Rationalisation of European Parliamentary Institutions, General Affairs Committee (Paul Struye, Belgium, Rapporteur), Doc. 91, June 13, 1958, p. 147.

"substitutes" or "successors elect" are not provided for in the Rome Treaty but are not explicitly precluded.

The Eden Plan as such has remained a dead letter. Although provision was made for exchange of information and liaison, the organic links between Little and Greater Europe contemplated in the British proposal were never established. The basic reason was to be found in a conviction among continentals that could hardly have been more clearly expressed than it was by the London Economist when it wrote:

> If there is the slightest chance of France, Germany and Italy setting up genuine political institutions to control common economic and defence policies, then British attempts to modify them in order to preserve the larger Council of Europe would be ill-advised. The Council has been a useful piece of scaffolding, without which the structure of unity would have taken shape more slowly; but it should not impede the growth of the permanent structure. British cooperation in technical bodies like the coal-steel pool and the defence community can be assured by special arrangements, but British political interests are best safeguarded by giving thought to the shape of the Atlantic community of which the European confederation will be a part.[8]

The difficulty with the Eden Plan lay not in some inherent defect of the two-tier principle but in the fact that the latter can be expected to work only when there is no inherent conflict between the two tiers. Notwithstanding the assurances of Eden, the belief persisted that organic ties between the Six and the non-Six would inevitably hamper the evolution of the European Community. In denying that the proposal had any such purpose, as a Labour spokesman told the Assembly, Eden had "robbed the Eden Plan of any real meaning. If Britain cannot intervene to correct the balance within the continental Community, then the form of her association with it is comparatively unimportant, and in fact it does not matter whether the continental Community is then built within the Council of Europe or within the Schuman Plan. . . ."[9]

---

[8]September 13, 1952, p. 607.

[9]Denis Healey in Council of Europe, Consultative Assembly, 4th Session, Official Report of Debates, September 18, 1952, p. 392.

The Eden Plan would probably have failed even if the underlying motives had not been subject to question. Its other central defect lay in the assumption that common, if tiered, institutions could be made to serve organizations committed to such different principles of operation as the supranational and the intergovernmental.

THE "GRAND DESIGN"

A second attempt to rationalize European institutions was the "Grand Design" put forward by Foreign Secretary Selwyn Lloyd at a meeting of the North Atlantic Council in December 1966.[10] Unlike the Eden Plan, the Grand Design confined itself to proposals affecting only the international parliamentary bodies. In common with the Eden Plan, however, it sought, in a more tentative way, to include the Six-nation assembly in its structure. In May 1957 the proposal was presented to the Consultative Assembly by David Ormsby-Gore, the Minister of State.[11] From that speech and a Foreign Office Memorandum that was given limited circulation in April,[12] the following outline of the Grand Design emerged.

A "General Assembly for Europe" would be established in Paris or Versailles to replace all of the existing bodies (Common Assembly, WEU Assembly, Consultative Assembly and NATO Parliamentarians' Conference), or as many of them as possible. The Assembly would have five commissions of differing membership, functions and procedures: Political, Economic, Defense, Social and Cultural, Legal and Administrative. Each commission would receive annual reports from the intergovernmental agencies in its field of competence.

Through the commissions, in short, a single assembly would be able to perform all parliamentary functions at the levels of the European Community, Greater Europe and the Atlantic Community. The arrangements would be flexible and informal enough to permit the accommodation under one roof

---

[10]In the meantime an important degree of rationalization had been achieved within the Six with the establishment of a single Court and a single Assembly to serve the ECSC, Euratom and the EEC.

[11]Ibid., 9th Session, May 1, 1957, p. 73-79.

[12]"Scheme for a general parliamentary Assembly for Europe," April 5, 1957, hereinafter referred to as Foreign Office Memorandum.

of the supranational Community, the European neutrals and the North Americans. A single secretariat would serve all commissions and the Assembly as a whole. Relations with the intergovernmental agencies would be unwritten, with the possible exception of the obligation of the latter to submit annual reports. The commissions would address their recommendations and questions directly to the agencies and/or the governments, but the latter would have no more than a moral obligation to reply and none to comply. Ministers could attend commission sessions, and joint meetings of executive bodies and the appropriate commissions could be arranged. If the six-nation assembly or assemblies were unwilling to lose their identity in such a structure, they should at least cooperate with the General Assembly and use the same headquarters and facilities.

The Grand Design as conceived in the Foreign Office Memorandum concerned the effectiveness of the institutions serving European and Atlantic cooperation. The proposal was to streamline the parliamentary wing with a view, at least ostensibly, to reducing duplication of effort and confusion in the public mind.

While the objectives of the proposal were in tune with a major preoccupation of the Consultative Assembly, the method was seriously questioned, principally for three reasons: it failed to propose a comparable rationalization of the executive agencies; its multiple-tier theory struck many continental federalists and representatives of the neutrals as unworkable; and the proposed informality of relations with the executive agencies would abandon ground already won by the Consultative Assembly and to a far greater extent by the WEU and Common Assemblies. Little was heard of this proposal following the debate in the Consultative Assembly.[13]   An Italian proposal contemplating the retention of the WEU, Consultative and Common assemblies, but with maximum identity of membership and a joint annual session, suffered a similar fate.[14]

---

[13]Council of Europe, op. cit., May 1-3, 1957. Cf. WEU Assembly, Proceedings, 3d Session, "European Assemblies: The 'Grand Design,'" General Affairs Committee (J. M. van der Goes van Naters, Netherlands, Rapporteur), Doc. 45, April 5, 1957; and ibid., "The Unification of European Assemblies," Doc. 62, September 21, 1957.

[14]Giuseppe Dardanelli, Council of Europe, op. cit., May 3, 1957. Cf. WEU Assembly, "Document covering the study by the Council of WEU

THE WIGNY AIDE-MEMOIRE

In 1959 Pierre Wigny, then Foreign Minister of Belgium, put forward a series of proposals designed to correct the "anarchy" of overlapping and conflicting activity among selected organizations. The proposals were submitted in an Aide-Memoire addressed to the Member States of the Council of Europe, following a decision by the Committee of Ministers of the Council of Europe on December 15, 1958, to study the possibilities of rationalization.[15]

The Wigny plan proposed in essence a new division of labor among the executive and parliamentary organs of NATO, OEEC, WEU and the Council of Europe; it made no attempt to reduce the number of bodies or to modify the existing statutory arrangements. Coordination would be further improved by increasing so far as possible the extent to which the national delegations in each body comprise the same individuals.

What was then the OEEC would be given parliamentary supervision by means of "ad hoc meetings" attended by the delegates of the Consultative Assembly of the Council of Europe and observers from Portugal and Switzerland and "possibly" Canada and the United States.

The functions of the Assembly of Western European Union would be taken over by the Consultative Assembly of the Council of Europe and the NATO Parliamentarians' Conference. In consequence, the WEU Assembly "would meet in future only to satisfy the requirements of Article 9 of the amended Brussels Treaty" and would have "very little to do."[16]

---

of the rationalisation of European Assemblies," 3d Report of Council to Assembly, Doc. 79, Appendix I, February 21, 1958; and ibid., "Rationalisation of European Parliamentary Institutions," Doc. 91, June 13, 1958. These reports of the General Affairs Committee (M. Paul Struye, Belgium, Rapporteur) offer some analysis of the British and Italian proposals and conclude that both were premature.

[15]The Wigny memorandum is cited above in Chapter 4, note 27.

[16]Ibid., p. 6 and 8. Article 9 provides that the WEU Council shall make a report on its activities, particularly in the field of arms control, to the WEU Assembly.

The NATO Parliamentarians' Conference, whose procedure and practice would be "brought into alignment" with the
rules of the Consultative and WEU Assemblies, would special-
ize in military and "general political" questions. The Consultative Assembly of the Council of Europe would continue to
deal with cultural, scientific, social, legal and administrative
questions; it would take up political matters of concern only
to Europe — for example, European integration. The OEEC
"Conference" would handle all economic questions.

A similar division of labor would apply to the ministerial
councils, whose respective calendars and agendas would be
worked out by a Coordination Committee. The OEEC Council
and the Committee of Ministers of the Council of Europe
would meet in joint sessions.

The Wigny proposal contemplated that more sweeping reforms, regarded as undoubtedly necessary, might be adopted
later, on the basis of the experience gained in carrying out
these "provisional" changes. Only one of the main recommendations, however, has been put into effect thus far. In
April 1959, the economic and social functions of Western
European Union were transferred to the Council of Europe.[17]
As will be seen in subsequent chapters, other aspects of the
proposal have been largely overtaken by events.

THE ROBERTSON PROPOSALS

In advancing a plan in 1959 for the rationalization of European institutions,[18] Dr. A. H. Robertson of the Council of
Europe Secretariat had proposed four basic principles: that
the six-nation Community must be omitted from consideration
because of the supranational links it was developing; that the
Atlantic Alliance or Community must also be omitted because
the common objective of the nations concerned is not unification but partnership and because its military purpose is not
shared by the European neutrals; that any politically acceptable plan must provide for the rationalization of intergovernmental as well as interparliamentary institutions; and that
the smaller regional organizations should be omitted as being

---

[17]Above, Chapter 4, note 27.

[18]European Institutions, op. cit., p. 232-245.

too specialized in purpose or too limited in membership to require attention in this context.

Robertson's proposal in essence called for: a merger of the Council of Europe and what was then the OEEC; the transfer of WEU's social and cultural functions to the Council of Europe (subsequently, as noted above, fully achieved); and the assignment of the WEU military activities to 7-nation sessions of the appropriate NATO bodies. This would include the defense deliberations of the WEU Assembly, which Robertson suggested should be transferred intact to the NATO "framework." Such transfer would, in that context, inevitably contribute, Robertson believed, to a gradual accretion of influence and powers by the NATO Parliamentarians' Conference.

Robertson's proposal was aimed essentially at streamlining the institutions of "Greater Europe." An assembly with a wider competence would be confronted with a single ministerial council having powers at least equal to those of the OEEC Council and a competence extended to embrace that of the OEEC, the Council of Europe and four other agencies (the Conference of Ministers of Transport, the Civil Aviation Conference, the Customs Cooperation Council and the Organization for Nuclear Research).

The multiple-tier principle is inherent in both major aspects of this plan. Within NATO it would facilitate execution of the military functions of Western European Union; within the new structure of Greater Europe, it would permit any adjustment that might be necessitated by the fact that two members of the OEEC (Switzerland and Portugal at that time) were not members of the Council of Europe. As to these countries, Robertson argued that, "It should not be at all difficult so to conceive the merger as to permit them to participate in all the activities of the unified organization, if they wish, and yet to refrain from participating in some of those activities should they so desire; thus they might not take part in the work of the Assembly or might limit their participation therein to certain selected subjects, such as the economic, and perhaps the social and cultural, discussions." [19]

As will be suggested below, this scheme for rationalization had much to commend it in 1959, but, like the Wigny proposal, it was soon to be overtaken by events.

---

[19]Ibid., p. 237.

AMALGAMATION OF THE COUNCIL OF EUROPE
AND OEEC/OECD

The Consultative Assembly has recommended on several occasions beginning in 1951 a merger of the Council of Europe and the OEEC. The intergovernmental character of the two organizations and their virtual identity of membership made the proposal seem natural. The advantages from the Assembly's point of view would be considerable: It would gain a direct relationship with an agency having a definite mandate and certain powers of decision and enjoying greater government support and public prestige than the ministerial organ of the Council of Europe. In a merger, the OEEC Council could retain its powers and extend them to those areas of cooperation presently assigned to the Committee of Ministers of the Council of Europe. The Committee of Ministers itself would disappear. The idea was revived in a report by E. de la Vallée Poussin of Belgium in 1958.[20] In April 1959 a Special Committee called by the Committee of Ministers submitted a report on the problems of rationalization, and the Foreign Ministers, in their 24th Session on April 20, 1959, decided as a first step toward closer ties with the OEEC to invite Swiss and Portuguese M.P.'s to attend debates in the Assembly on OEEC reports and economic questions.[21]

Further action was deferred pending the outcome of the negotiations in the OEEC for establishment of a Free Trade Area in Greater Europe. These discussions had begun on February 13, 1957, and came to an abrupt end with the French announcement on November 14, 1958, that a Free Trade Area was "not possible."[22] On July 31, 1961, Prime Minister Macmillan announced Britain's intention to seek membership in the Common Market. The ensuing negotiations were terminated on January 14, 1963, at General de Gaulle's press conference. Thus, throughout the period from early 1957 until

---

[20] Council of Europe, Consultative Assembly, Communications on the Rationalisation of European Institutions, Doc. 776, January 14, 1958. Cf. ibid., Report on the Institutional Reform of the Council of Europe (H. Teitgen, France, Rapporteur), Doc. 763, December 20, 1957.

[21] Switzerland joined the Council of Europe in 1963.

[22] Le Monde, November 16–17, 1958.

the end of 1962, questions of rationalizing existing institutions in Europe were largely in abeyance while efforts to establish closer economic links between the Six and the Outer Seven ran their course.[23]

---

[23]On February 1, 1962, an elaborate "arrangement" was approved between the Council of Europe and the OECD, in effect continuing and refining the relationship between the former and the OEEC. It provides inter alia for the exchange of reports, joint sessions of liaison committees, reciprocal attendance of observers at appropriate meetings, submission of written questions to OECD by Representatives of the Assembly, and presentation of the OECD reports to the Assembly in person by an OECD minister.--Arrangement between the Council of Europe and the Organization for Economic Cooperation and Development, approved by the OECD Council on January 9, 1962, and by the Committee of Ministers of the Council of Europe on February 1, 1962 (Resolution (62) 4), Strasbourg: November 1962.

7 RATIONALIZING INTERPARLIAMENTARY CONSULTATION— CURRENT ALTERNATIVES

The establishment of the OECD on October 1, 1961, introduced a new factor into the problem of rationalization and gave impetus to proposals for the establishment of a consultative Atlantic Assembly having competence in the field of economic cooperation as well as that of collective defense. Prospects for a rationalization on that basis, on the other hand, were adversely affected by the indefinite suspension in January 1963 of the negotiations for Great Britain's admission into the European Community. In the eyes of many Europeans, the setback to the European movement gave new importance to the work of both Western European Union and the Council of Europe. It is clear nevertheless that the problem of strengthening and rationalizing interparliamentary consultation continues to be regarded as an important item of unfinished business by the NATO Parliamentarians' Conference, the Assembly of Western European Union, and the Consultative Assembly of the Council of Europe. Four proposals — those put forward respectively by Pierre Pflimlin, John Lindsay, Arthur Conte and Thorkil Kristensen — comprise the currently available options.

THE KRISTENSEN PROPOSAL

Since 1960, when agreement on establishment of the OECD was reached, the Consultative Assembly has repeatedly and unavailingly recommended that members of parliament from those OECD states that are not associated with the Council of Europe should meet with the Assembly with a view to serving as an advisory body to the OECD.[1] In June 1962 the Secretary General of the OECD, Thorkil Kristensen, proposed as an alternative that the governments of the OECD countries

---

[1] There are now five OECD members not members of the Council of Europe — Canada, Portugal, Spain, the United States, and (since May 5, 1964) Japan.

convene a special parliamentary conference to discuss the work of the Organization, the conference to be composed of from two to five M.P.'s from each Member country. His proposal contemplated that the body might become permanent, thereby adding a seventh international parliamentary consultative assembly to the existing array.[2]

On September 25, 1962, however, the Consultative Assembly reiterated the conviction that its discussions of OECD would have "greater significance" if the Americans and Canadians took part, and it issued a warning that "the creation of OECD must not give rise to the setting up of a new international parliamentary assembly, whether official or unofficial, as there are, from the European point of view, the most serious objections to the creation of a special new assembly which would be in addition to existing parliamentary assemblies and would result in a dissipation of effort injurious to Europe." The Recommendation considered the Kristensen proposal acceptable only if the Consultative Assembly "in some way or another" were to represent the Members of the Council of Europe.[3]

---

[2]These developments are reviewed in a report by Pierre Pflimlin and Alois Zimmer (Doc. 1546), an Explanatory Memorandum accompanying a Draft Resolution of January 15, 1963. The explanatory memorandum is hereinafter cited as the Pflimlin–Zimmer memorandum. The idea of creating an OECD Parliamentary Conference has also been sponsored by Rep. Henry S. Reuss (D. Wisc.) whose Concurrent Resolutions in the 87th and 88th Congress would set up subcommittees of the House Foreign Affairs Committee and the Senate Foreign Relations Committee to explore the matter. (H. Con. Res. 425, 87th, 2d, Feb. 19, 1962, and H. Con. Res. 87, 88th, 1st, Feb. 7, 1963.) See also U. S. Congressional Record, May 17, 1963, p. 9058; and Off Dead Center: Some Proposals to Strengthen Free World Economic Cooperation, A Report to the Joint Economic Committee, 89th Congress, 1st Session, December 1965, p. 19, submitted by Representatives Reuss and Robert F. Ellsworth (R. Kans.).

[3]Council of Europe, Consultative Assembly, Texts Adopted, Recommendation 336, September 25, 1962. The generally negative response to Kristensen's proposal led him to suggest, unavailingly, an alternative — that small delegations from OECD countries attend a single ad hoc meeting just before the NPC's 1963 session, to discuss development assistance and other OECD matters. The question of a second meeting or a permanent organization would be deferred.

The decision of the NATO Parliamentarians' Conference of November 16, 1962, to study the establishment of a consultative Atlantic Assembly capable of serving both NATO and the OECD, posed a challenge for the Consultative Assembly.[4] In January 1963 the Assembly consequently authorized the appointment of a delegation to seek the cooperation of the Committee of Ministers and the Member Governments in persuading the United States and Canadian Governments to support the Assembly's proposals for ad hoc meetings between the Assembly and parliamentarians of those two countries. The delegation was also empowered to establish direct contacts later if necessary with the U. S. Congress and the Canadian Parliament with a view to concluding and implementing an agreement by which such meetings would in effect become the parliamentary consultative arm of the OECD.[5] On May 10, 1963, the Assembly further directed its delegation to "give urgent consideration" to the recent proposal of Senator Fulbright for the establishment of a consultative Atlantic Assembly.[6]

As their respective agenda and resolutions make clear, the Consultative Assembly and the NPC have staked out rival claims to competence in OECD matters. The Consultative Assembly, its then President, Pierre Pflimlin, has pointed out, is "the only European Assembly that is specifically committed to concern itself with OECD; it represents the largest

---

[4]Although the NPC has at least temporarily abandoned that particular project, its desire for greater influence over the OECD remains undiminished. In 1964 the NPC adopted a resolution noting that its invitation to the non-NATO members of OECD "to send observers" had been declined, and recommending "that the President of the Conference emphasize to the Secretary General of the OECD, the advantage to be gained from closer co-ordination between the work of OECD and that of the Economic Committee."--NPC, Reports and Recommendations, 10th Session, November 16-21, 1964, p. 61.

[5]Resolution 241, originating as a proposal of the Political Committee in Doc. 1546, January 15, 1963.

[6]Order No. 217, to the Bureau of the Assembly, May 10, 1963, Council of Europe, Consultative Assembly, Orders Adopted, May 1963, p. 3. Sen. Fulbright's proposal was made in the second of his Clayton Lectures on "A Concert of Free Nations" at the Fletcher School of Law and Diplomacy, Tufts University, April 29-May 1, 1963.--J. William Fulbright, Prospects for the West (Cambridge, Mass.: Harvard University Press, 1963), p. 64-66.

number of European countries, including the neutrals."[7] Being now the master of its own agenda, it can be expected to continue its practice of debating OECD reports and formulating recommendations about them. It is, moreover, clear that the Consultative Assembly will resist strongly, at least until such time as Britain and other EFTA countries may be admitted to the European Community, any suggestion that it should be "rationalized" out of existence.

To Pflimlin and many of his associates, the NPC suggestion that Atlantica needs only a European parliament and a consultative Atlantic Assembly is at best "a long-term solution."[8] Meanwhile, the Assembly may be expected to regard itself as being, in the words of a 1963 Recommendation, "more capable than any other organization of creating a truly European public opinion" and as being needed in Europe primarly for that reason.[9] As to the relative merits of its and the NPC's rival claims to competence in OECD matters, the Consultative Assembly, Pflimlin points out, has two further advantages: First, it already exists as an official body; secondly, not being concerned with NATO military questions, the Assembly "may inspire confidence in the newly developing countries" to whom a large measure of the OECD's work is devoted.[10]

THE PFLIMLIN "TWO-ASSEMBLY" PROPOSAL

Early statements and resolutions appear to have created some confusion as to how the Consultative Assembly proposes to modify Atlantic parliamentary consultation.[11] Whatever

---

[7]Pflimlin-Zimmer Memorandum, op. cit., p. 7.

[8]Ibid., p. 6.

[9]Council of Europe, Consultative Assembly, Texts Adopted, Recommendation No. 356, May 8, 1963.

[10]Pflimlin-Zimmer Memorandum, op. cit., p. 7.

[11]The evidence of confusion has emerged mainly in oral and written reports, that cannot be cited, of discussions between European and American legislators.

may have been the original intent, it is now clear that the Assembly is not seeking to incorporate North American delegations into the Council of Europe for purposes of OECD debates. Its purpose, rather, is to arrange for a periodic dialogue between European and North American legislators on non-military Atlantic issues, most of which comprise OECD business.

In pursuing this objective on behalf of the Consultative Assembly, Pflimlin put forward a new proposal in 1963.[12] It is one of two proposals currently under serious consideration as alternatives to (or precursors of) a consultative Atlantic Assembly.

The plan contemplates that the OECD parliamentary sessions, perhaps taking the form of an "Atlantic Assembly for Economic and Social Affairs," would be convened for a few days (two to five, for example) immediately following (or preceding) a session of approximately equal length of the NATO Parliamentarians' Conference. (The latter might be organized, possibly by action of the North Atlantic Council, as an "Atlantic Assembly for NATO.") While countries would be free to appoint their representatives to the new body as they wished, the plan suggests in effect that the European members designate all or part of their Strasbourg delegations and that the others accredit to the new body all or part of their NPC delegations.

---

[12]The Pflimlin proposal is set forth in Council of Europe, Aide-Memoire Concerning the Organisation of Parliamentary Debates among Representatives of the Member Countries of OECD, Doc. 1721, September 20, 1963. (Cited hereinafter as Pflimlin Aide-Memoire.) This document recognizes that the proposed meetings "cannot be organised within the framework of existing institutions."---p. 3-4. Cf. Joseph Harned, "Atlantic Assembly --- a Genesis," Atlantic Community Quarterly, Vol. 3, No. 1, Spring 1965, p. 43-49. In 1964 the NATO Parliamentarians' Conference for the first time recognized that the Pflimlin proposal might prove more practicable in the immediate future than any alternative, when it adopted a recommendation that "discussions among parliamentarians be undertaken looking toward the creation of an Atlantic Consultative Assembly, or assemblies meeting concurrently, embracing to the greatest degree possible the membership of the North Atlantic Treaty Organisation and the Organisation for Economic Co-operation and Development."---NPC, Reports and Resolutions, 10th Session, November 16-21, 1964, p. 53 (emphasis supplied). Karl Czernetz, Chairman of the Foreign Affairs Committee of the Austrian Parliament, member of the Socialist Party Bureau and a representative to the Consultative Assembly, is credited as one of the principal originators of the "two-assembly" proposal.

Staff for the meetings on economic and social affairs would be provided from the secretariats of NATO, the OECD and the Council of Europe, and could include persons designated by the United States and Canada. Such an arrangement is seen as helping assure adequate coordination between the new organization and the older assemblies.

The Pflimlin formula has the practical advantage of associating the Council of Europe (through the proposed identity of individual participants) with the economic and social sessions, as the Consultative Assembly had insisted, while at the same time meeting American objections to holding such sessions under the aegis of the Council of Europe. A further advantage is that by maintaining a complete juridical separation between the sessions dealing respectively with military and economic questions, the full participation of the European neutrals in the new organization is presumably facilitated.

The proposal contemplates that the OECD Council could take the initiative in organizing the economic assembly. This would assure the official character of the new entity, while avoiding the difficulties and delays that would almost certainly ensue if the arrangements were to be undertaken by means of a new treaty or protocol.

The principal weakness of the plan is undoubtedly that in effect it creates another consultative assembly without necessarily eliminating any of the existing bodies. At least some advocates assume that the work of the "Atlantic Assembly for Economic and Social Affairs" would eventually encompass that of the Consultative Assembly of the Council of Europe. Whether this would happen is likely to depend upon several imponderables, notably the extension of the European Economic Community to Britain and others of the "outer Seven." It might depend also on the ability of the successor organization to assume the Consultative Assembly's functions in the fields of cultural and legal cooperation, human rights and refugees — something not contemplated at the outset by the Pflimlin proposal.

Some advocates of the plan argue that the resulting proliferation would be more apparent than real. Proliferation of delegations is avoided, as noted above, through the identity of individual participants. Thus the addition of an Assembly for Economic and Social Affairs would increase, not the number of participants required, but only the time demanded of some of the present parliamentary delegations. In regard to the

question of imposing a greater burden on the time of participants, supporters of the Pflimlin proposal suggest that this
would not be a serious factor for the Strasbourg delegations
because it is to be assumed that the session of the new assembly would supplant, or largely supplant, one of the three
annual part-sessions of the Consultative Assembly — the other
two dealing with strictly European regional affairs. As to the
delegations from the non-members of the Council of Europe,
partisans of this proposal point out that its implementation
need impinge no more heavily on their time than would proposals looking toward wider competence and correspondingly
longer sessions of the NATO Parliamentarians' Conference.

Assuming that representation in the proposed Atlantic
Assembly for Economic and Social Affairs is governed by the
"Strasbourg formula," the national delegations (other than that
of the United States) need not vary from their present strength.
To the extent, however, that the European delegations to the
Consultative Assembly and the NPC are not identical, or are
not designated en bloc to the new assembly, competition for
seats and a problem of selection could arise. Similarly, those
not included in the delegations to the new assembly might be
inclined to resist any eventual effort to reduce the competence of the two older bodies.

Those who urge this proposal believe that it is the only
practicable way to establish without delay a broadly based
European-American parliamentary dialogue on problems of
the Atlantic "partnership." The recent soundings taken in
Europe by Pflimlin and by NPC delegates reportedly indicate
that any attempt now to establish the new assembly by means
of a formal statute will encounter decisive opposition from
the French and the British governments. Moreover, it is
argued, only a complete juridical separation between the
military and the other functions would enable the European
neutrals to take part, and some European members of NATO
are believed to be unwilling to join an OECD parliamentary
forum in which the neutrals would feel unable to participate.
Finally, at least some advocates of the Pflimlin plan believe
that its implementation would pave the way for further rationalization and for the eventual establishment of a single Atlantic
Assembly.

Resistance to the Pflimlin proposal appears to have come
mainly from some American legislators, who believe that
Congress would consider any further proliferation of international assemblies to be inadmissible. There has also been

some feeling that it would be unnecessary and unwise to adopt a more cumbersome structure merely to accommodate the neutrals, and that it would be preferable to move, when possible, directly to an all-embracing consultative Atlantic Assembly, open to the neutrals on a take it or leave it basis.

Whatever the merits of that view, the Pflimlin proposal clearly is based on two assumptions that have yet to be fully substantiated: first, that the desired debates can be arranged only at the expense of adding one more assembly to the present array — i.e., that no higher degree of rationalization can or should be sought in present circumstances; and, secondly, that the European neutrals would settle for nothing less than complete juridical separation of the parliamentary organs in which the questions of Western defense and the questions of Western economic and social cooperation would be considered. As will be suggested in Chapter 9, there is some evidence that neither of those propositions is entirely justified.

Parliamentarians have temporized with the problems of interparliamentary rationalization for a decade. Before new, long-term commitments for further temporizing are made, legislative leaders on both sides of the Atlantic might well consider whether a more satisfactory alternative should not be thoroughly explored. This, however, need not preclude interim attempts to strengthen the NATO Parliamentarians' Conference, nor need it preclude an interim, informal arrangement permitting members of the NATO Parliamentarians' Conference and the Consultative Assembly to meet periodically for discussions of OECD and other appropriate matters. In May 1965, the latter concept was endorsed for the first time by key American members of the NATO Parliamentarians' Conference. Such joint sessions might well provide the best possible framework and sponsorship for the effort to achieve a more definitive system of interparliamentary consultation in the Atlantic Community.

THE CONTE PROPOSAL

Arthur Conte, French M.P., NPC participant and a past President of the WEU Assembly, presented his "Draft Protocol to the North Atlantic Treaty" to the Seventh NATO Parliamentarians' Conference (1961). This would establish an Assembly of the Atlantic Alliance composed of representatives appointed by the national parliaments and authorized "to deliberate concerning the state of Western defence and security." The Assembly would meet in September in Paris and in March in Quebec or Washington. It would receive oral and written reports from the North Atlantic Council, put written questions to the Council, appoint committees of investigation, draw up its own budget, and express its views through recommendations or opinions which it could transmit directly to governments, national parliaments and international organizations. Conte proposed a link of sorts between the new assembly and that of WEU by providing in Article XI of his draft protocol that the Representatives of the WEU Assembly "may constitute a restricted session of the Assembly in order to deliberate on defence matters of essentially European interest. They shall meet immediately following or preceding the Sessions of the full Assembly, in particular to consider the Annual Report submitted to them by the C o u n c i l of Western European Union. . . ." The Assembly would draft its own budget, subject to agreement of the North Atlantic Council and would issue recommendations or opinions on the annual NATO budget.

As noted in Chapter 3, this concept was revived in the 1965 session of the NATO Parliamentarians' Conference and is now under consideration in the Political Committee.[13]

THE LINDSAY REPORT ON A CONSULTATIVE ATLANTIC ASSEMBLY

Two groups of the NATO Parliamentarians' Conference — the officers of the Political Committee and the Special Subcommittee on "Institutionalisation" created in November 1962 — worked independently in the spring and summer of 1963 on the question of rationalizing Atlantic parliamentary organization and came up with quite different recommendations. While the Subcommittee's soundings at the various

---

[13]The Conte proposal appears in NPC, Draft Additional Protocol to the North Atlantic Treaty [n.d.]. Cf. NPC, Speech by President Arthur Conte to the North Atlantic Convention of NATO Nations, Paris, January 1962. Cf. Noël Salter, Aide-Mémoire relatif á l'Assemblée de Défense Occidentale (WEU Doc. A/P 796) July 14, 1958), which advocates in effect a merger of the WEU Assembly and the NPC into a single defense assembly and proposes for the purpose draft protocols to the Brussels and NATO Treaties and adaptations of the charter and procedure of the WEU Assembly.

Foreign Offices eventually led it to decide that the project
was not politically feasible and should be deferred, the work
of the officers of the Political Committee led to the presentation in November 1963 of a favorable report (by John V.
Lindsay, then Congressman and the Rapporteur) that had to
be drastically revised before it could be approved by the full
Committee and adopted in plenary.[14]

The first official draft of the Political Committee's report[15] expressed the view that "parliamentarians of the Atlantic nations, including the membership of both NATO and
the OECD, acting independently of all existing parliamentary
bodies, including the NATO Parliamentarians' Conference,
should organise themselves forthwith to take positive steps
toward the creation of a consultative Atlantic Assembly to
serve as a parliamentary body for both NATO and the OECD."
This draft proposed, for "purely illustrative" purposes, a

----

[14]The episode reflected both a failure of coordination and a diver-
gence of opinion. The officers of the Political Committee — Lord Ogmore
(U. K.), Chairman; Nils Langhelle (Norway), Vice Chairman; and John V.
Lindsay (U. S.), Rapporteur — met first in London, March 1-2. The full
Committee in June approved the continuation of the study by its officers,
directed the Rapporteur to draft a report on its behalf for the November
1963 session, and resolved that it should be the recipient also of the
Special Subcommittee's report. The Subcommittee met first in Paris
on March 21 and established a Working Group comprising the officers
of the Subcommittee: Viggo Hauch (Denmark), Chairman; Lord Silkin
(U. K.) and Wayne Hays (U. S.), Vice Chairmen; Lucien Radoux (Belgium)
and Michel Boscher (France), Rapporteurs. The Working Group met in
Copenhagen April 26 and June 29 and in Paris May 27. The Subcommittee
in effect decided to submit recommendations not on the charter of a consultative Atlantic Assembly as stipulated in its terms of reference but
on the political feasibility of establishing such an assembly. In short,
the Subcommittee had decided to disregard its terms of reference, while
the Political Committee had proceeded to act upon them. As a result the
Standing Committee unexpectedly found itself confronted in November
with two contradictory reports and the necessity of making a choice. It
endorsed the Subcommittee's view, and the Political Committee's report
was rewritten to conform with the dominant view that the hour of the
Atlantic Assembly had not yet struck. (NPC, Minutes of the Subcommittee, March 21, June 29 and November 1, 1963; Minutes of the Working
Group, April 26, May 27 and June 29, 1963; Meetings of the Standing
Committee, July 1 and November 4, 1963.)

[15]NPC, Draft Report of the Political Committee, 9th Session, Doc.
F. 126, PC(63)28, Paris, October 1963.

unicameral assembly composed of from 100 to 200 M.P.'s and apportioned among member states according to population. To accommodate the neutrals, the work would be divided among five committees and between two distinct plenary sessions. The first of these, of about four days' duration, would deal with military and political matters relating to NATO; the second, of about equal length, chastely separated from the first by a weekend, would deal with economic, social, scientific and human rights questions, with the non-NATO members of OECD fully participating. The proposed assembly, it was suggested, might have "at the minimum" the following powers:

> the right to have regular reports from NATO and OECD; the right to submit questions and receive either answers or formal refusals to answer from the Councils and Secretaries General of these two organisations; the right to invite representatives of the Councils and the Secretariats of NATO and the OECD to appear before the Assembly or its appropriate committees for questioning and to have such invitations either accepted or formally refused; the right to submit recommendations to the two organisations and after a proper interval of time require reports on actions taken or not taken as a result of the Assembly's recommendations.

A further power might be to express, by simple majority or perhaps a two-thirds vote, the Assembly's "confidence or lack of confidence in specific actions or decisions of the two executive bodies." The draft expressed the belief that a consultative Atlantic Assembly "can and should be created in the near future" and that a formal treaty would not be required for the purpose.

The substance of these proposals was never debated by the Conference or its Political Committee. By the time the Committee met to take up the report in November, the conclusions of the Subcommittee had been circulated. These were essentially that the time was not ripe for an effort to create an Atlantic Assembly and that the NPC should confine itself to measures aimed at improving its performance rather than changing its status or powers.[16] After considerable

---

[16]The basis for this conclusion about the creation of an Atlantic Assembly is considered in Chapter 9. The internal reforms adopted at the Ninth Session of the NPC are reviewed in Chapter 2.

discussion,[17] the Committee acceded to the Subcommittee's position. The Committee's draft, as one member remarked, would become a useful source at a more propitious time.

AN ADAPTATION OF THE NATO
PARLIAMENTARIANS' PROPOSAL

The three broad alternatives for the further development of interparliamentary consultation that are currently subject to any serious consideration are those of M. Conte (1961), of the Council of Europe (1963) and of the NATO Parliamentarians' Conference (1962). While the NPC deferred action on the Lindsay recommendations of the following year, it explicitly left them in the category of unfinished business. Meanwhile, the NPC will consider in 1966 the proposal of Sir Geoffrey de Freitas in effect to revive the Conte project for a NATO Consultative Assembly.

As has been suggested above, the Council of Europe or Pflimlin plan has the advantages and the disadvantages of an expedient. In order to hasten the establishment of a broader base for interparliamentary discussion of OECD business, it leaves intact the four existing international assemblies and in effect creates another.

The NPC concept of 1962, on the other hand, which was derived in part from a recommendation of the Atlantic Convention of NATO Nations, would in effect sacrifice the prospect of immediate reform in the interest of eventually attaining a more rational realignment of interparliamentary functions and reducing the number of assemblies from four to two.

The recommendation of the Atlantic Convention of NATO Nations for parliamentary rationalization was:

> ... that the NATO Parliamentarians' Conference be developed into a consultative Atlantic Assembly, to meet at stated intervals, or upon the call of its President or otherwise to receive reports regularly transmitted to it by the Secretaries General of other Atlantic bodies;

[17]NPC, Meeting of the Political Committee, Paris, November 5, 1963 (Doc. F. 190, PC (63) 34), p. 2-7.

to raise questions for and to consider, debate and review the work of all Atlantic institutions, and make recommendations to other Atlantic bodies and governments on questions of concern to the Atlantic Community. A permanent secretariat and an annual budget should be provided for the Atlantic Assembly to ensure continuity. In certain defined cases, recommendations should be by weighted majority vote. Members of the Atlantic Assembly would be selected by member governments in accordance with their constitutional procedure. They need not necessarily be Parliamentarians. The members thus chosen would have the power to elect a limited number of additional members of equal status.[18]

In its own resolution on the subject, adopted in 1962, the NATO Parliamentarians' Conference welcomed that recommendation, reaffirmed its "dedication to the task of building a genuine Atlantic Community " and:

States its conviction that only two international parliamentary bodies for the Atlantic nations are needed, one a Parliament for a United Europe and the other an Assembly for the Atlantic Partnership, and that the present various European institutions should conform with this pattern which should come about not by the creation of new bodies but by the evolution from existing ones;

Recommends in addition to appropriate action by National Governments the appointment by the President of the NATO Parliamentarians' Conference with the advice and recommendation of the Standing Committee and the Political Committee of a special subcommittee of the Conference to study and submit recommendations, with the assistance and counsel of the Atlantic Institute, on the following:

(1) a constitution or charter for a consultative Atlantic Assembly as called for by the Declaration of Paris and in accordance with the Preamble to that recommendation;

(2) the precise powers and functions to be exercised by such a consultative assembly;

---

[18] Declaration of Paris, op. cit., Part I, para. B-2.

(3) a form of association with the Organisation for Economic Cooperation and Development or, alternatively, a Consultative Atlantic Assembly to serve, and so constituted as to enable it to serve, as a single consultative parliamentary body both for the North Atlantic Treaty Organisation and for the Organisation for Economic Cooperation and Development with due consideration being given to such special arrangements as may be necessary with regard to the membership and participation of those nations which are members either of NATO or of the OECD but not of both.

(4) the creation of a Permanent High Council at the ministerial level to plan, concert, and, in defined cases, to determine policy on matters of common concern to the Atlantic Community, as called for by the Declaration of Paris; the creation of an Atlantic High Court of Justice with jurisdiction over legal disputes arising from the interpretation and application of treaties, as called for by the Declaration of Paris; and the creation of an Atlantic Council for youth, education and culture, as called for by the Declaration of Paris; so far as these three matters affect the constitution and functions of a consultative Atlantic Assembly.[19]

There is a certain neatness and plausibility about the NPC's notion that the existing consultative bodies should "evolve" into a single assembly for European union and another for Atlantic cooperation. Further work by the NPC in that direction has been "temporarily" deferred for political reasons. Such intrinsic merit as that conception may have had can of course be appraised independently of the political developments that have sidetracked it. If it is inherently sound it may be revived at a propitious time. The theoretical case for it depends in part on a showing that all the necessary consultative functions could be performed in that framework, i.e., that the remaining institutions between them could be functionally related to all existing and prospective regional development within the area. The proposition would be invalid, for example, if it appeared that neither the assembly of the European Community nor the

---

[19]NPC, op. cit., 8th Session, November 12-16, 1962, p. 47-48. Resolution adopted unanimously on November 15, 1962.

assembly of Atlantic cooperation could deal appropriately with prospective developments among the nations of "Greater Europe," i.e., Western Europe of "the Seventeen."

That Greater Europe needed its own parliamentary structure was of course an assumption of Robertson's plan. His plan had undeniable merit in 1959. As Robertson himself noted, the opportune moment for putting it into effect would be upon the creation of the Free Trade Area. The policies and development of the proposed Free Trade Area might quite logically have been added to the agenda of the Council of Europe. The defeat of that project, however, reduced the prospects of "Greater Europe" as such. The subsequent establishment of the OECD reduced them further by putting its kind of economic cooperation on an Atlantic rather than a European basis. The application of Britain for membership in the European Community struck a further blow at the concept of "Greater Europe" as a framework and method of regional cooperation by suggesting that from then on the thrust would be not to develop the intergovernmental cooperation of "Greater Europe" but to enlarge the supranational Community. By the beginning of 1963 it seemed clear that "Greater Europe" as a framework and method had been overtaken by events and that all notions for rationalizing its structure or enhancing its influence were doomed henceforth to fall between the two stools of the European Community and the Atlantic partnership.[20]

This need not mean necessarily that the perennial forecasts of the atrophy of the Council of Europe have been vindicated. So long as the Europe of the Six and the Europe of the Seventeen remain unable to agree on a single structure and technique of unification, a common assembly on the Strasbourg model will continue to have its raison d'être. And so long as the Atlantic parliamentary body remains neither equipped nor disposed to deal effectively with the issues now dealt with at Strasbourg, that consultative function will continue to be provided by the Council of Europe.

---

[20]In a thoughtful "new definition of the role of the Council of Europe," Secretary General Peter Smithers has pointed out that the problem of unity among Council members is now "essentially that of the relationship of the rest of Europe... to the European Community" and has proposed a "planned programme of harmonisation" by means of "parallel or analogous inter-State agreements" that would orient the activities of members "in the same direction even if they were proceeding by different methods."---European Co-operation: A New Definition of the Role of the Council of Europe, Statement by the Secretary-General (Strasbourg: May, 1965).

The notion of only two assemblies advanced by the NPC presupposes in effect the merger of the Consultative Assembly with either the European Parliament or some form of consultative Atlantic Assembly and the absorption by the latter of the NPC and the WEU Assembly. A merger of the two European entities was evidently implied in the proposal of the NATO Parliamentarians' Conference, and, as noted, will presumably remain sidetracked until Britain and other EFTA nations are allowed to join the Six.

The remaining theoretical possibility for a rationalization into two assemblies would be a merger involving the Consultative Assembly, the WEU Assembly and the NATO Parliamentarians' Conference. There is at present little disposition among European parliamentarians to affect a rationalization on that basis, and as will be seen it would require the prior resolution of several difficult problems.[21]   On the other hand, it would clearly not preclude the eventual enlargement of the European Parliament to the boundaries of Greater Europe, and it would, if implemented, entail certain advantages — notably a major reduction of overlapping functions and an extension of the parliamentary consultative process to the work of OECD. This theoretical alternative may therefore usefully be examined. It breaks down into two questions — first, a reassignment of WEU Assembly functions and secondly, a consolidation of the NPC and Consultative Assembly in some new form of consultative Atlantic Assembly.

Reassignment of WEU Assembly Functions

The broad questions involved in transferring the executive and parliamentary functions still exercised by WEU

---

[21]Sentiment among American NPC participants is divided. Among the more active members, Congressmen Wayne L. Hays had indicated skepticism, while Senator Fulbright and former Congressman John Lindsay are on record in favor of a broadly competent consultative Atlantic Assembly. (Senator Fulbright cited above, footnote 6, Chap. 8.) Regarding Representative Hays' view, see his remarks before the Consultative Assembly of the Council of Europe—op. cit., Official Report of Debates (Doc. AS(16) CR 14) November 6, 1964, p. 52–55. In May 1965 Congressman Hays and Senator Fulbright gave their support to proposals for a joint meeting of members of the NPC and of the Consultative Assembly, and the first such encounter may occur as early as November 1966. They also supported the idea of participation by U. S. delegations in regular meetings of the Consultative Assembly. The first such meeting took place in Strasbourg, May 3–6, 1965.

were considered in Chapter 4. While formulas may vary, the desirability of such a transfer is clear.[22] The defense deliberations of the WEU Assembly relate essentially to NATO business and might better be handled in a parliamentary forum that includes all members of the Alliance. On the other hand, it is doubtful that the NPC could do justice to that additional assignment without a substantial increase in its staff and budget. If the organs of Western European Union were to suspend activity, their staff and budget might well be transferred to the NATO framework. That budget, proportionately augmented by the United States and the other NATO countries not members of WEU, would assure the Atlantic parliamentary body relatively substantial additional resources at relatively little additional cost to members.[23]

Another contribution WEU might bring to an Atlantic parliamentary body, as noted in Chapter 4, lies in the realm of methods and procedures.

Merger of the Consultative Assembly and the NPC—a Consultative Atlantic Assembly

By the criteria suggested at the beginning of Chapter 6, there is much to be said for a consolidation of the Consultative Assembly and the NPC into a consultative Atlantic Assembly. Except for a handful of states, the membership is identical. The method of work — advice and exhortation to stimulate intergovernmental agreement — is the same in each. The objectives, essentially those of mutual understanding and closer cooperation (among comparably homogeneous nations), are very similar. The areas of "competence" overlap in all but the military sphere, and even there the difference has been

---

[22]The need for a reassignment of WEU functions has been recognized, in broad outline at least, by other students of the subject, e.g., Kenneth Lindsay, European Assemblies, op. cit., and Towards A European Parliament, op. cit., p. 144. Also P. E. P., European Organisations, op. cit., p. 226-228, 349-350; Claxton, op. cit.; and esp. Wigny Memorandum, op. cit.; Timothy W. Stanley, NATO in Transition: The Future of the Atlantic Alliance (New York: Frederick A. Praeger, 1965) p. 397-398.

[23]Under the NATO cost-sharing formula (above, footnote 11, Chap. 2), the eight non-WEU NATO members would contribute 35.54%. If the contribution of the WEU members remained unchanged, the new budget might be approximately $700,000, or more than three times that of the NATO Parliamentarians' Conference.

narrowed in practice by the fact that the Consultative Assembly freely debates and advises on the "political implications" of defense problems. As has been noted, the continued existence of the two assemblies will almost certainly mean continued duplication of efforts to oversee the work of the OECD.

The whole process of Atlantic unification would be accelerated to the extent that the agreements and conventions of Greater Europe could be extended to the United States and Canada. Such extension would be facilitated by a consolidation of the two assemblies and the appropriate executive agencies. On the other hand, this need not interfere with those states that might wish to proceed more rapidly in certain types of cooperation. Insofar as the U. S. or any other member government felt unable to enter into certain proposed joint undertakings, the others would be free to go ahead on the basis of a device developed at Strasbourg known as the partial agreement. Under this arrangement, the Committee of Ministers proceeds as follows:

> If the Committee, by the unanimous vote of the representatives casting a vote and by a majority of the representatives entitled to sit on the Committee, decides that abstention from participation in any proposal before it shall be permitted, that proposal shall be put to the Committee; it shall be considered as adopted only by the representatives who then vote in favour of it, and its application shall be limited accordingly.

> Any additional expenditure incurred by the Council in connection with a proposal adopted under the above procedure shall be borne exclusively by the Members whose representatives have voted in favour of it.[24]

---

[24]Resolution adopted by the Committee of Ministers at its 9th Session, August 1951, text in Council of Europe, Consultative Assembly, Doc. 60, November 26, 1951, p. 573. Cf. OECD Treaty (Art. 6): "Each Member shall have one vote. If a Member abstains from voting on a decision or recommendation, such abstention shall not invalidate the decision or recommendation, which shall be applicable to the other Members but not to the abstaining Members." Manlio Brosio, NATO Secretary General, has made the following comment on the partial agreement: "The principle is an excellent one, and I should like to see it implemented to the greatest extent possible. But it has its limitations; and these begin to operate when the new proposal is such as to raise fundamental political difficulties for those who object to it."---NPC, Plenary Verbatim, 10th Session, November 16, a.m., 1964, p. 13.

While resort to that procedure requires unanimous consent, the procedure itself offers a useful exception to the unanimity rule in cases where some Members may wish neither to participate nor to prevent others from participating in a particular project. The device has been used but seldom in the Council of Europe — it was invoked for the first time in 1956, five years after the rule was adopted — but would probably find more frequent application in a consultative Atlantic Assembly.

A further argument in support of consolidating the two Assemblies is that European unification is a legitimate concern, indeed a major objective, of the West as a whole. The U. S. Government and Congress have given significant support to that movement since the Marshall Plan. To the extent that a Western organization outside the Six can influence the policies and evolution of the European Community, it may well be that an organization — particularly a parliamentary one — representing the Atlantic Community as a whole could serve that purpose more effectively than one confined to Greater Europe. This would seem a reasonable proposition whether or not the British Government continues to seek admission to the European Community and whether or not France continues to resist it.

The Principal Difficulties

If the proposition for a merger of the Council of Europe and a reorganized NPC has a certain rational appeal, it has also some serious practical difficulties. Briefly stated, at least three conditions would have to be met: A formula would have to be found for accommodating (or leaving out) the European neutrals, whose policies — although evolving — permit cooperation only in the economic, social and cultural spheres; the assembly would have to be assured a staff and budget sufficient to permit longer sessions than those of the NPC, more frequent committee meetings and more nearly adequate research, documentation and conference services; and a means would have to be found of reconciling the greater demands on the time of the participating parliamentarians with the fact that many of them have already, in the NPC, approached the limits of the time they can afford to divert from national and local responsibilities. These are essentially political problems and will be further considered in the last chapter. It may however be preferable to consider here the purely organizational aspects of associating the European neutrals.

Association of the European Neutrals

The fact that the neutrals of Europe are prepared to co-operate with other Western countries in some fields but not in others inevitably complicates the reorganization of Atlantic parliamentary consultation. As John Lindsay stated the problem in his report to the Eighth NPC:

> The neutral countries of Europe have constantly refused to participate in any activities including parliamentary associations which consider questions of defense and security. Yet they participate as full members of OECD and are active in many important international economic issues. On the other hand, Atlantic parliamentary relationships are rendered less effective if their competence is limited to either security or economic welfare or if these two inseparable problems are to be dealt with by two independent parliamentary bodies. Some form of association satisfactory to neutral parliamentarians must be found.[25]

To this end of associating the neutrals, a variety of two-tier formulas have been suggested: a single Assembly of twenty nations, with a defense committee composed solely of NATO-country representatives and provision for separate plenary meetings to discuss defense committee reports; a single assembly holding two distinct but consecutive sessions, the second being confined to NATO members and military matters; a single assembly having two chambers with distinctive titles; two juridically distinct assemblies meeting consecutively in the same place and having separate secretariats.

Under such arrangements, the neutrals might be full members of the organization (in the case of the last, full members of only one of the two assemblies). As an alternative, or in conjunction with any of these formulas, the neutrals could no doubt be offered an associate-member status

---

[25]NPC, Reports and Recommendations, 8th Session, November 12-16, 1962, p. 9.

if that would facilitate their participation, with the option of converting it to full membership at any later date. Of these alternatives, as noted above, the officers of the NPC's Political Committee (Lord Ogmore, United Kingdom, Chairman; Niles Langhelle, Norway, Vice Chairman; and John V. Lindsay, U. S., Rapporteur) concluded early in 1963 that a tiered-committee arrangement with separate plenary meetings would be both preferable and acceptable.

The association of the European neutrals might in principle be achieved under one of several possible formulas that would offer them varying degrees of insulation from the defense activities of a consultative Atlantic Assembly. Whether any such formula is likely to encourage their participation — a far more difficult question — will be considered in the last chapter.

CONCLUSIONS

The idea of strengthening interparliamentary consultation by streamlining present arrangements and establishing a consultative Atlantic Assembly has, as will be shown more fully in the last chapter, gained wide support among parliamentarians and government officials over the past four or five years. Views differ less on the need than on the timing of possible next steps in that direction. In principle, the optimum rationalization of the present interparliamentary consultative arrangements would replace three of the six assemblies with one. The new entity would be a consultative Atlantic Assembly organized on some variant of the two-tier formula to embrace all or most OECD nations and authorized to assume all functions of the NATO Parliamentarians' Conference, the Consultative Assembly of the Council of Europe and the Assembly of Western European Union.

This would eliminate the main sources of overlapping function and put the spotlight more sharply on the two parallel but interacting regional movements within the area — those of European integration and Atlantic partnership. At the same time, the revised system could be sufficiently flexible to permit and indeed promote varying degrees of cooperation among different groupings of the member states (for example, through adoption of "partial agreements"), and it need in no way impede an eventual extension of the European Community to the "outer Seven."

The following chapter presents a profile or model of a consultative Atlantic Assembly as it might emerge if based on such an "optimum" rationalization of existing arrangements. Because of certain political obstacles, considered in the final chapter, it is likely that this can be attained, if at all, only after an experimental interim phase during which the European-American parliamentary dialogue may be developed on a less formal basis.

8   A CONSULTATIVE ATLANTIC ASSEMBLY

Virtually all those who have expressed themselves in favor of transforming the NATO Parliamentarians' Conference envisage that the new Atlantic body would be purely consultative.[1] Any who believe that the Atlantic nations are ready for a more advanced form of interparliamentary institution should no doubt accept the burden of proof. In its full sense, however, "consultative" means not only that the body may give advice, but also that its advice will be sought and fully considered by the governments and intergovernmental agencies. For this reason there is wide though not unanimous agreement among students of the subject that the proposed Assembly should be created by an international treaty or agreement that would clearly define its competence and powers and its relationship to the intergovernmental bodies concerned. Many but by no means all of those who have studied the matter believe also that an Atlantic Assembly should be open to all members of OECD (with perhaps special status for Japan) and that it should be competent to deal with all matters of common concern — political, military, economic, social, cultural, scientific.

SELECTION AND QUALIFICATIONS OF PARTICIPANTS

Participants in the NPC, the Consultative Assembly of the Council of Europe and the European Parliament are generally selected by and from the national parliaments on the basis of

---

[1]Notably: Atlantic Convention of NATO Nations; the 1962–1963 officers of the Political Committee of the NPC; Strausz-Hupé et al., op. cit., esp. p. 290-299; Livingston Hartley; Philander P. Claxton, Jr.; Senator Fulbright; Christian Herter; Arthur Conte. Cf. NPC Draft Rules of Procedure for a Consultative Atlantic Assembly, F. 50, PC (63) 17(Annex); NPC, L. Radoux, "Introductory Note to a Report on the Proposal for the Creation of an Atlantic Consultative Assembly" (E.32) April 5, 1962; NPC, Subcommittee, An Atlantic Assembly, The Secretariat, February 1963 (F. 10 PC (63) 1); and Senate Committee on Foreign Relations, Problems and Trends in Atlantic Partnership, II, Staff Study, Doc. 21, June 17, 1963, p. 47-49.

consultation among the non-Communist party leaders. The WEU Assembly is composed of its seven Members' delegations to the Consultative Assembly. Originally, the authority to name participants in the Consultative Assembly was assigned to the governments, but this was changed to assure the Assembly greater independence, and it appears widely agreed that the present method is preferable to any other.[2] There is little support for the idea of choosing a purely consultative Atlantic Assembly by popular election, although that method would simplify the problem of American participation (assuming a prohibition of dual mandates) and would entail electoral campaigns that might contribute to public understanding of world problems. Indeed, as noted above,[3] there are plausible misgivings as to the wisdom of the popular election even in the case of the European Parliament. By that reasoning, any attempt initially to elect an Atlantic Assembly would seem clearly premature.

There is a wider difference of opinion as to whether (assuming no popular election) all participants should be members of national parliaments. Some believe that this question should be left to decision at the national level.[4] They emphasize that the possibility of appointing some non-parliamentarians would give the U.S. Congress needed flexibility in arranging for American participation in appropriate numbers. It has been pointed out that this would be analogous to the procedure for choosing members of the United States Senate prior to adoption of the Seventeenth Amendment of the U.S. Constitution in 1913. The analogy is faulty, as Claxton notes, because the Senate, once elected, did not have to rely on its influence with the state legislatures in order to assure implementation of its resolutions.[5] Those opposed to the mixed delegation emphasize that the influence of the Assembly would

---

[2]The Atlantic Convention of NATO Nations, however, proposed that the Atlantic Assembly "be selected by member governments in accordance with their constitutional procedures." Since generally the governments could be expected to defer to the legislatures, the practical effect of that wording might prove little different.

[3]Chapter 4. See also Roy Price, op. cit., p. 89.

[4]E.g., Atlantic Convention, Claxton, Hartley, Paul Van Zeeland. (The latter is cited in NPC Secretariat, "An Atlantic Assembly," February 1963, p. 16.)

[5]Op. cit., p. 88-89.

be diluted and that non–M.P. participants would be less representative of people, purse strings, or power. [6]

There is something to be said, however, for leaving the
choice to the national parliaments. An undue weakening of
the Assembly's influence could be prevented by stipulating
for example (a) that not more than a third of a national delegation may be non–M.P.'s; (b) that the latter shall be co-opted
by the parliamentary delegation or appointed by the speakers;
and (c) that the non–M.P.'s shall be persons who have achieved
national distinction in one or more of the fields of activity
represented by the Assembly's committees or falling within
the Assembly's competence.

Provision should be made on the same basis for the appointment of alternates. Renewal of national delegations
should take due account of the desirability of assuring continuity while exposing a growing number of national M.P.'s
to the experience of interparliamentary activity. The principle might well be stated in the rules, but in such a way as
to avoid tying the hands of the national legislatures by a rigid
formula.

REPRESENTATION OF MEMBERS

Suggestions for the size of the Assembly tend to fall within
the range of 100 to 200. There is general agreement that the
apportionment of seats should be at least roughly related to
population but that each Member should have a minimum of
three representatives. These principles are already firmly
established in the practice of the existing European assemblies,
as is the concept of one vote for each delegate. An assembly
of fewer than 100 would compel an increased distortion of the
delegate–population ratios and would impose unduly narrow
limits on the access of M.P.'s to the interparliamentary experience. An assembly larger than 200 is usually felt to be
unwieldy, although the European Parliament, when elected by
universal suffrage, will number 426, and there are other
precedents — for whatever they may prove — on the national
level.

---

[6]This is the view of some NPC participants, including the 1962–63
officers of the Political Committee.

Representation in the Consultative Assembly of the Council of Europe is based on an approximate ratio of one delegate for 3 million inhabitants. This may be compared in Table 5 with other ratios. The Strasbourg formula in turn determines representation in three other bodies — the Assembly of Western

Table 5
Selected National Parliaments and the European Parliament
(Electoral Plan)
Compared as to Number of Seats and Inhabitants Per Seat[a]

	National Parliaments		European Parliament		
	No. of Seats	Inhabitants per Seat	No. of Seats	Inhabitants per Seat (Proposed) Transitional Stage	Final Stage
Belgium	212	42,703	42	323,322	215,548
France	552	81,649	108	625,972	415,315
West Germany	497	106,245	108	733,389	488,926
Italy	596	82,270	108	697,569	465,046
Luxembourg	52	6,154	18	26,666	17,778
Netherlands	150	74,580	42	399,534	266,357
Average	-	81,913	-	593,860	395,913
United States	535	344,878	-	-	-

[a]Adapted from P.E.P., Direct Elections and the European Parliament, Occasional Paper No. 10, October 24, 1960, p. 8.

European Union, in which the seven Members are represented by their Consultative Assembly delegations; the European Parliament, in which the six Members send delegations just twice the size of their Consultative Assembly contingents; and the NPC, in which voting strength (but not the number of participants) of the European Members is the same as their representation in the Consultative Assembly. The composition of the European Assembly when popularly elected will also be based on the Strasbourg formula, since each of the six delegations will then be just three times its present size.

Under the Strasbourg formula, the United States would have to have a delegation of 60 to 70 — a size generally felt to be impracticable. Most proposals contemplate that the U.S., whose representation in the NPC today is limited by Congressional resolution to 18, could not authorize a delegation of more than 40 to 50 and would therefore have to accept substantial underrepresentation. If, however, as the experience of the other assemblies suggests, voting in the Atlantic Assembly follows individual or partisan rather than national patterns, and so long as the action taken is merely advisory, the underrepresentation will have less practical significance than might otherwise be the case. A requirement of qualified majorities for important issues would provide further insurance against any ill-effects of such distortions.

Table 6 relates the present apportionment arrangements in four assemblies (columns III-VI inclusive) to 1960 population figures and percentages (columns I and II). Column VII presents an apportionment based on the Strasbourg formula plus, where that is not applicable, the NPC formula. Column VIII suggests a possible apportionment of seats in a consultative Atlantic Assembly based on the Strasbourg formula. The OECD countries are listed in descending order of population totals.

The apportionment of seats in the proposed Assembly on the basis of the Strasbourg formula has two disadvantages. It would call for some sixty American participants, which might be difficult even if part of the delegation were appointed from non-members of Congress. Secondly, it yields a total number of participants that is somewhat larger than might be desirable. On the other hand, extension of the Strasbourg formula has the political advantage of preserving the present Council of Europe representation of 16 of the 20 prospective Members. A larger total number also permits less discrepancy between the underrepresentation of the larger countries and the overrepresentation of the smaller countries. In preliminary discussions among the 1962 officers of the NPC Political Committee, consisting of Lord Ogmore (United Kingdom), Nils Langhelle (Norway) and John Lindsay (United States), an assembly of approximately 185 seemed preferable. Within that total, the U. S. would have 48 delegates, the European Big Four would each have 20, Spain 9, Turkey 8, Canada 5, with the others having 4, 3 or 2 each. This however would increase the distortion considerably, as Table 7 suggests.

In either case, representation will be severely disproportionate so long as it is based on national states of such divergent sizes. Within the range of these alternatives, the choice is necessarily somewhat arbitrary.

Table 6
OECD Countries' Representation in Selected Assemblies

Country[a]	I Population (Millions)	II % of OECD Area's Population	III Council of Europe	IV NPC (Votes)	V WEU	VI European Parliament Now	VI European Parliament Elected	VII Strasbourg NPC Combined	VIII Atlantic Assembly
United States	185.2	34.6		36				36	60
West Germany	54.4	10.1	18	18	18	36	108	18	18
United Kingdom	52.9	9.9	18	18	18	36	108	18	18
Italy	49.8	9.3	18	18	18	36	108	18	18
France	46.2	8.6	18	18	18	36	108	18	18
Spain	30.6	5.7						(10)	10
Turkey	28.6	5.3	10	10				10	10
Canada	18.4	3.4		12				12	8
Netherlands	11.7	2.2	7	7	7	14	42	7	7
Belgium	9.2	1.7	7	7	7	14	42	7	7
Portugal	9.2	1.7		5				5	7
Greece	8.4	1.6	7	7				7	7
Sweden	7.5	1.4	6					6	6
Austria	7.1	1.3	6					6	6
Switzerland	5.5	1.0	6					6	6
Denmark	4.6	.9	5	5				5	5
Norway	3.6	.7	5	5				5	5
Ireland	2.8	.5	4					4	4
Luxembourg	.3	.1	3	3	3	6	18	3	3
Iceland	.2	--	3	3				3	3
TOTALS	536.2	100.00	141[b]	172	89	142	426	204	226

[a] Japan, a member of OECD, is not represented in any of the existing assemblies.
[b] Add Cyprus' 3 representatives for complete total of 144.

Table 7
Illustrative Ratios of Representatives to Population Under
Strasbourg Formula and an Alternative Formula

	Strasbourg formula (extended — 226 reps)	NPC Officers formula (185 reps)
U. S. A.	1 : 3.1 million	1 : 3.8 million
France	1 : 2.6 million	1 : 2.3 million
Luxembourg	1 : 0.1 million	1 : 0.15 million

One close student of the subject suggests an Assembly of from 193 to 203 participants, which he arrives at by modifying the Strasbourg formula to assign the United States only 40 to 50 representatives. He would deviate further from the Strasbourg formula by reducing Spanish and Portuguese representation to about half of their "Strasbourg" entitlement — from 10 to 5 in the case of Spain and from 7 to 4 in the case of Portugal. He argues that such a reduction "seems only reasonable when the degree of representation provided by the Spanish and Portuguese parliaments is considered." An alternative, he suggests, would be "to allow each country a basic representation of 2 or 3 and additional representation based not on population, but on votes cast for parliamentarians in the most recent elections."[7] A further alternative might be to provide for associate membership. In the Council of Europe, associate members were represented in the Assembly but not in the Committee of Ministers (Statute, Art. 5). In a consultative Atlantic Assembly, associate membership might entail the right to speak but not to vote. For political reasons, the question of Spanish participation may prove academic for some time to come.[8]

FUNCTIONS AND POWERS

Advocates of an Atlantic Assembly generally assume that it should be consultative and should be authorized to deal with all matters of common concern to Members, both within and

---

[7]Source has asked not to be identified.

[8]See Chapter 9 below.

beyond the area. They are similarly agreed in regard to the Assembly's functions, which are to initiate public debate on important issues; to render opinions or recommendations with respect to those issues; to review and debate the work of NATO and OECD and, on its own initiative or on request of those bodies, to issue opinions or recommendations thereon. To the extent that the Assembly might take over the functions of the Consultative and WEU Assemblies, its review function would be extended to other organizations.

To perform those functions, the Assembly is felt to require most or all of the following powers: (1) to determine its own agenda; (2) to receive annual or more frequent reports from NATO and OECD; (3) to put questions in writing to those agencies and to receive either answers or formal refusals to answer; (4) to invite representatives of the Councils and Secretaries General to appear in person to answer questions or present statements before plenary or committee meetings and to have the invitations either accepted or formally refused; (5) to obtain reports from the executive agencies on the actions taken or not taken by them in response to Assembly recommendations; (6) to submit its opinions and recommendations in the appropriate languages directly to all Member governments, the parliaments, the press and to all appropriate international agencies; (7) to draw up its own budget for approval of the Members; (8) to meet in regular session, and in special session upon its own initiative or that of its officers, as well as that of the executive agencies; (9) to adopt its own rules of procedure within the framework of an international treaty or agreement.

There appears to be little sentiment in favor of giving the Assembly a right of censure comparable to that of the European Parliament. That power is applicable indeed to a type of organ not present in the Atlantic structure as such, namely the executive commissions, whose defined powers are exercised independently of the Member Governments and in the interest of the Community as a whole. Lord Franks has elicited much interest with his proposal for

> ...a new organization, institution or commission, which will have sufficient standing, independence and initiative to formulate common solutions and put them forward to the governments of the several nations of the group, so that they will have to face in argument not merely each other but also and at the same time

the solution proposed for the partnership as a whole as best realizing its common good.[9]

Were such a body to come into existence, particularly if it had powers of decision as well as recommendation, its tenure might well be made to depend upon the confidence of the proposed Assembly.

Meanwhile, the Assembly's authority to review, criticize, advise and publicize would constitute a right of moral censure that should help assure its actions the respectful attention of the executive agencies. Whether that right might on occasion be expressed in the form of a "motion to disagree" to an annual report, as in the WEU Assembly, ought to be carefully considered by those charged with drafting the Atlantic body's statute and rules.[10] Including such a provision would provide the advantage of formalizing and emphasizing the procedure while at the same time, presumably, defining and limiting the manner in which it can be invoked. Similarly, as in the WEU Assembly,[11] the resolutions adopted with respect to reports of the executive agencies might gain in status and impact if defined and treated as the "replies" of the parliamentary body to the executive agency.

As the experience of the other assemblies has suggested, the effectiveness of an advisory body lacking the power of subpoena and investigation must depend in part on the regularity, pertinence and thoroughness of the reports it receives. Adequate reports would enable the Assembly to gain a comprehensive understanding of the work of the executive agency. They would bring before the Assembly specific questions on which parliamentary consultation is desired, and they would inform the Assembly as to the action taken or not taken on its previous recommendations. Experience also indicates that the Assembly can rely on receiving such reports only if it is endowed with official status and that much depends upon spelling out the nature and extent of the reporting obligation.

Other aspects of the relations between the Assembly and the executive agencies — notably the questions of joint meetings,

---

[9]Lord Franks, "Cooperation Is Not Enough," Foreign Affairs, Vol. 41, No. 1, October 1962, p. 33.

[10]See Chapter 4 above.

[11]See Chapter 4 above.

liaison committees, the presence of Ministers at Assembly meetings and visits of inspection — should also be explicitly dealt with in the statute or rules.

STRUCTURE—COMMITTEES

It is likely that in performing its functions, a consultative Atlantic Assembly will need a more elaborate committee structure than that of the NATO Parliamentarians' Conference. Whether standing committees should be stipulated in its charter or, as was the case with the Consultative Assembly, left to the Assembly's discretion, is relatively unimportant except insofar as the committee structure may be affected by any multiple-tier arrangement designed to accommodate the European neutrals.

The committee structures of the NATO Parliamentarians' Conference, the Consultative Assembly, the WEU Assembly and the two main executive agencies are set forth in Table 8 (that of the European Parliament being omitted because its more specialized functions do not lend themselves to useful comparison with the others).

If the Atlantic Assembly is to be organized to deal with the OECD and NATO and to handle matters of internal administration and procedure, it may find its minimum and initial roster of permanent committees — some with sub-committees — to be approximately as follows:

1. Political Committee

2. Defense Committee

3. Economic and Social Committee

4. Cultural and Information Committee

5. Scientific and Technical Committee

6. Procedure, Privileges & Credentials Committee

7. Administrative and Budgetary Committee

Table 8
Permanent Committees of Selected Regional Organizations

	NATO	OECD	NPC	Consultative Assembly	WEU Assembly
1.	Political Affairs (includes information)	Scientific and Technical Personnel	Political	General Affairs	General Affairs
2.	Military (under Council, not Sec. General)	Economic Policy	Military	Cultural and Scientific	Defense Questions and Armaments
3.	Production and Logistics	Balance of Payments	Scientific and Technical	Economic	Budgetary Affairs and Administration
4.	Scientific Affairs	Development Assistance	Economic	Social Questions	Rules of Procedure and Privileges
5.	Economics and Finance	Manpower and Social Affairs	Cultural Affairs and Information	Agriculture	
6.		Industry		Legal and Administrative	
7.		Agriculture		Rules of Procedure and Privileges	
8.		Nuclear Energy		Population and Refugees	
9.				Local Authorities	
10.				Nations not in Council of Europe	

VOTING AND THE CONDUCT OF BUSINESS

The unit rule or weighted national vote in the NPC's current voting arrangements is inherently inconsistent with the concept of parliamentary consultation. As has been suggested above,[12] it has "worked" so far only because the resolutions of the NPC have not generally engendered controversy in any important measure among either individuals, party groups or national delegations. There is broad agreement among the advocates of a consultative Atlantic Assembly that each delegate should be uninstructed, have one vote and vote as an individual. The one-man one-vote concept presupposes that representation will be at least roughly proportionate to population, although as has been shown above, the latter principle will be severely distorted in practice so long as the parliamentary "districts" are national states of such divergent sizes.[13]

There appears also to be little question but that the voting requirements should distinguish between procedural and substantive questions and that any motion to censure or even to disagree should entail still stricter procedures. The present main provisions in the four Assemblies are set forth in Table 9.

In three of the four assemblies, qualified majorities are required on substantive matters. This principle is peculiarly appropriate for consultative bodies, whose recommendations, not having binding force, must depend for their effectiveness not only on their inherent merit and timeliness but on their ability to attract broad support. The exception is the European Parliament, where only an absolute majority is required for substantive resolutions other than those embodying a motion of censure. In both that organization and the WEU Assembly, however, special majorities are required for motions, respectively, of censure and disagreement, and in addition each requires a waiting period (three days and one day, respectively) prior to the vote on such motions. The required majority for substantive resolutions in the NATO Parliamentarians'

---

[12]Chapter 2.

[13]Table 7.

Table 9
Voting Procedures in Four Parliamentary Assemblies

	NPC	Consultative Assembly	WEU Assembly	European Parliament
Substantive motions	2/3ds of votes cast if 2/3ds = at least 1/2 of total no. of votes of Assembly	2/3ds of votes cast comprising at least 1/3d of delegates of Assembly, with a majority present	Absolute majority of votes cast	Absolute majority of votes cast
Motions to censure or disagree	Not applicable — see above	Not applicable — see above	Maj. of membership — 45 of 89 votes (Same for amendment of Charter)	2/3ds of votes cast if the 2/3ds = majority of membership
Procedural motions; amendment of rules	Not specified	Absolute majority of votes cast. Applies also to resolutions not addressed to Committee of Ministers	Absolute majority of votes cast	Absolute majority of votes cast
Inclusion of items on agenda	Not specified	Same as substantive motions	Absolute majority of votes cast	Absolute majority of votes cast
Election of officers	Absolute majority of votes cast on 1st and 2d ballots; relative maj. on 3d	Absolute majority of votes cast on 1st and 2d ballots; relative maj. on 3d	Absolute majority of votes cast on 1st and 2d ballots; relative maj. on 3d	Absolute majority of votes cast on 1st and 2d ballots; relative maj. on 3d
In committees	Absolute majority of votes cast	Absolute majority of votes cast (on reports as a whole, maj. of committee must be present)	Absolute majority of votes cast (on reports as a whole, maj. of committee must be present)	Absolute majority of votes cast

Conference is two-thirds of the votes cast, providing the two-thirds equals at least one-half the total voting strength of the Conference. The need for a broad consensus, the disparities in delegate-"constituency" ratios, and the purely advisory character of the proposed Assembly's resolutions all militate in favor of retaining the essentials of that provision.

The practice of delegates' voting as individuals should no doubt be both encouraged and reflected by the seating arrangement. Neither the NPC practice of seating by national blocs nor the European Parliament's seating by political groups seems as appropriate for the proposed Atlantic Assembly as the Consultative and WEU assemblies' tradition of seating individuals alphabetically.

Several factors — the prospective size of the Assembly, the foreseeable length of its agendas, and the likelihood that the annual business of at least the plenary meetings must be completed in a comparatively brief session — make it highly desirable to build in reasonable limitations on the duration of debate. These traditionally include restricting the length and number of interventions on procedural questions, closing the list of speakers, enforcing the principle of germaneness, providing for closure of debate, and stipulating time-limits on speeches. Although most of these procedures are available in most of the assemblies, they have seldom been imposed, and when imposed, seldom rigidly enforced. The rules might be so cast, for example, as to make closing of the list and the imposition of time-limits the normal rather than the exceptional practice, with such derogations as the Assembly or its President may decide. Such draconian measures might be partly offset by a rule, à l'américaine, according representatives the right to extend their remarks for the record.[14]

While an unusual degree of discipline will thus be indispensable to success under the conditions in which a consultative Atlantic Assembly would be operating, the necessity

---

[14]Kenneth Lindsay rightly notes that "rules of procedure have been sometimes written in blood" and warns that "There are limits to dragooning parliamentarians and circumscribing free speech." -- European Assemblies, op. cit., p. 52 and 57. Cf. J. Allan Hovey, Jr., "Obstructionism and the Rules of the General Assembly," International Organization, August 1951, p. 515-530, and "Voting Procedure in the General Assembly," ibid., Vol. IV, No. 3, August 1950.

might well be made a virtue. Few who read the debates of the Consultative Assembly, which is the Atlantic Assembly's closest analogue as to size, scope and procedures, would question that more rigorous control of debate might do much for the sharpness, relevance, and public impact of the proceedings.

SITE AND SESSIONS

There is general agreement among advocates of a consultative Atlantic Assembly that its headquarters should be in Paris (or Versailles), the principal argument being that Paris is already the seat of NATO and the OECD. (The argument would of course have less force if President De Gaulle's recent announcement leads to a transfer of the NATO Council). A European site would be more convenient and economical than one in North America in view of the fact that some two-thirds of the delegates would be Europeans. It is frequently suggested, however, that like the European Parliament, the Atlantic Assembly — and certainly its committees — might well decide to hold occasional sessions in other capitals as a means of stimulating public awareness in other countries or areas. Strasbourg might become a strong candidate as the seat of the Atlantic Assembly if the Consultative Assembly should eventually be absorbed by the Atlantic Assembly. Strasbourg has the advantage of excellent existing facilities and an experienced staff for international assemblies. The fact that it is not a national capital would also be counted in its favor by many. On the other hand, Strasbourg's close identification with the European movement would be against it in the view of some, as would the fact that it is less accessible than a major capital.

Table 10 sets forth the sites and approximate lengths of sessions of the four assemblies:

Table 10
Sites and Sessions of Four Parliamentary Assemblies

	NPC	Consultative Assembly	WEU Assembly	European Parliament
Site of meetings	Paris	Strasbourg	Paris	Strasbourg
Length of sessions	5-6 days	1 month	6-8 days	30-40 days
Dates	November	In 2-3 parts fall & spring	First week of June and first week of December	In 6-8 parts including 3d Tuesday in October and 2d Tuesday in May

It is generally thought that the Assembly's sessions would
have to be at least twice as long as the five to six days now
taken by the NATO Parliamentarians' Conference. If the
Atlantic Assembly absorbs one or more of the existing assemblies, and if drastic new precedents are not established
for the streamlining of deliberations, even that estimate will
prove optimistic. Provision would presumably be made for
the holding of extraordinary sessions, and there have been
suggestions that these could be called at the behest of the
North Atlantic Council or the OECD Council as well as of
the Assembly or its steering committee. There have also
been suggestions for holding the annual session in two parts,
one in Europe and the other in the United States or Canada.

BUDGET AND STAFF

As has been noted, the wider responsibilities of an Atlantic
Assembly will necessitate a substantial increase in the budget
and staff now available to the NATO Parliamentarians' Conference. The need will be accentuated if the comparative
brevity of sessions compels greater than usual reliance upon
the secretariat. To assure optimum quality of staff, it is
often suggested that appointments should be made on the sole
basis of merit with little or no regard to nationality. Present
uncertainties as to the size of the assembly, the duration of
sessions, the scope of its responsibilities, and the number
of committees permit only a very general estimate as to the
prospective size of budget and staff. Since the Consultative
Assembly has more in common with the projected Atlantic
Assembly than do the others, its budget — some $5,000,000 a
year — may indicate a reasonable order of magnitude. While
the Atlantic body's sessions are likely to be shorter, any resulting economies may be offset by its larger size and the
greater distances to be travelled. Table 11 provides a rough
comparison of staffs and average budgets for the four existing
Assemblies:

Table 11
Staffs and Budgets of Four Parliamentary Assemblies

	NCP	Consultative Assembly	WEU Assembly	European Parliament
Staff[a]	5-10	430	26	450
Budget	$220,000	$4,900,000	$428,000	$5,600,000

[a]The figures for staff do not reflect the substantial temporary expan-
sion that occurs during assembly sessions. Neither staff nor budget figures reflect the additional services from which the European assemblies
benefit as a result of the activities of their respective executive agencies.

SUMMARY

As presently envisaged by most of its advocates, and within a considerable range of variation, the proposed Atlantic Assembly would be a purely consultative body of some two hundred persons designated by the parliaments of all or most of the OECD countries. It would meet in Paris or Versailles in an annual session of some two weeks' duration to review the work primarily of NATO and the OECD, to debate all issues of common concern to Members, and to adopt, by qualified majority, opinions and recommendations looking toward the resolution of common problems. Representation would be roughly on the basis of the Strasbourg formula, and participants would speak and vote as individuals. The Assembly would have maximum latitude to determine its own agenda, obtain reports from the executive agencies, put questions to Ministers and other executive authorities, and distribute its reports and recommendations. It would dispose of a staff and budget adequate to its purpose.

CHAPTER 9 THE POLITICS OF ATLANTIC PARLIAMENTARY CONSULTATION

Despite evident shortcomings, the interparliamentary as-semblies have exerted a demonstrable and salutary influence on both the formulation and the popularization of international policy. As an institution, the superparliament is undoubtedly here to stay. There is, however, general agreement among participants and observers that the mechanism is due for an overhaul — that there should be fewer assemblies and that their functions, methods, powers and competence should be redrawn. In particular, it has become clear that the "dialogue" between European and American legislators should be re-organized for greater efficiency and impact. To most of those who have expressed an opinion, this implies the establish-ment — at some point and in some form — of an official con-sultative Atlantic Assembly.

In the United States, this idea has gained strong bipartisan support in both the Executive and the Legislative branches of government, and is backed by the Atlantic Council of the United States, a national group of private citizens under the chairmanship of General Lauris Norstad. Dean Acheson has given the proposal full support. Senator Fulbright, long a leading participant in the NATO Parliamentarians' Confer-ence, has declared his belief that the establishment "in the near future" of a consultative Atlantic Assembly with compe-tence in both NATO and OECD affairs would be "a desirable and feasible measure for the strengthening of the Atlantic Community [and] would have a salutary effect in alleviating the current atmosphere of disunity and recrimination within the Alliance."[1] Former Congressman John V. Lindsay, another veteran participant in the NPC, is the author of one of the main proposals, reviewed above, for the establishment of such an assembly. Congressman Wayne Hays, a Vice Presi-dent of the NPC since its inception and President in 1956-57,

---

[1]J. William Fulbright, "A Concert of Free Nations," International Organization, Vol. XVII, No. 3, Summer 1963, p. 787-803. For Acheson's statement, see U. S. Senate, The Atlantic Alliance, Hearings before Sub-committee on National Security and International Operations, Committee on Government Operations, 89th Congress, 2d Session, April 27, 1966, p. 31-32.

has also endorsed the idea of a consultative assembly, although he opposed the Lindsay formula and has thus far given active support only to proposals contemplating less formal contacts between the American delegations and those of the Assembly of the Council of Europe. Senator Javits, the Chairman of the Economic Committee during the first decade of the NPC, has urged Congress to "take the lead" in support of this project on the ground that a consultative assembly "could have an enormous impact on creating a favorable atmosphere for a variety of vital trans-Atlantic issues, now deadlocked in view of Franco-American differences."[2] Vice President Humphrey told the eleventh session of the NATO Parliamentarians' Conference that "I think it [an Atlantic Assembly] is needed and I hope that it can be fulfilled."[3] It is no secret that the highest officials of the Department of State, while publicly deferring to the judgment of the legislators, have actively encouraged efforts in that direction.

The NATO Parliamentarians' Conference, although acknowledging the existence of obstacles to an early culmination of such efforts, has consistently and unanimously endorsed the objective. As the Political Committee reported in 1964,

... Now would seem to be the right moment for setting in motion the preparations for such an institution. ... European and North American legislators are not sufficiently involved in trans-Atlantic affairs. ... The people ... should have a reliable link with the trans-Atlantic business through their elected representatives. Indeed, the problem of holding the bureaucrats in this field accountable to parliamentary bodies should be a matter of concern not just to elected officials, but to the academicians, political journalists, and responsible citizens in all of the Western democracies. First and foremost, European and North American parliamentarians should be able to explore the full range of their joint concerns — political, military, commercial, monetary, development, etc. — within a broadly representative institution possessing consultative powers. Such institution should be well within the reach of the countries concerned.[4]

---

[2]Senator Jacob K. Javits (R., New York), "The New Battle of Britain," speech in the Senate, Congressional Record, August 12, 1965, p. 19423.

[3]Vice President Hubert H. Humphrey, NPC Verbatim Report, 11th Session, October 5, a.m., 1965, p. 3.

[4]NPC, Reports and Recommendations, 10th Session, November 16-21, 1964, p. 13.

How such an institution is to be brought about is a matter of less general agreement. Different evaluations of the technical and political obstacles have led to a variety of proposals as to the form, the tactics and the timing. Some would convert the NPC into a consultative Atlantic Assembly for both NATO and OECD, perhaps leaving empty chairs for the European neutrals and any others unwilling to join at the outset. Some would simply give the NPC official status, thereby enhancing its facilities and powers without enlarging its competence. Others would establish an assembly or conference for the OECD, thereby increasing the number of interparliamentary assemblies. Still others, like John Lindsay, would construct a consultative Atlantic Assembly on some variant of the two-tier principle, in the belief that this would permit the neutral countries of Europe to join. Finally, those, like Pierre Pflimlin, doubting that the neutrals could participate on such a basis, have proposed in effect that representatives of the NPC and of the Consultative Assembly of the Council of Europe meet together immediately before or after the NATO Parliamentarians' annual session to discuss OECD affairs.

ATTITUDES OF GOVERNMENTS TOWARD THE ATLANTIC ASSEMBLY IDEA

Of the various alternatives, only that proposed by Lindsay in 1963 attempts to reconcile the objective of a single broadly competent Atlantic Assembly with the objective of appropriate participation of all or virtually all nations of the Atlantic Community. The NATO Parliamentarians have so far given more attention to this proposal than to any of the others. As has been noted above,[5] they warmly endorsed the concept in 1962 and 1963 but concluded in the latter year that it could not immediately be implemented.

The study undertaken by the NPC's Special Subcommittee in 1963 — while, as will be seen, open to criticism — provided some useful insights into the political obstacles, and hence into the ultimate prospects and possible next steps.

With regard to the three neutrals — Austria, Sweden and Switzerland — Michel Boscher, one of the Subcommittee's

---

[5]See Chapters 1 and 7.

Rapporteurs, reported them as willing "to participate in an Assembly of a non-military nature."[6] A similar view was given the Subcommittee by the Secretary General of OECD, who suggested however that even the name Atlantic might cause difficulties for some of the neutrals. He advised also that most developing countries "would be wary of accepting aid from an Organisation with an Atlantic label as, in their opinion, 'Atlantic' was still, and would remain tied to NATO."[7]

The main opposition to the idea of a consultative Atlantic Assembly was reported to have come from the governments of France and the United Kingdom. Edward Heath, then President of the Board of Trade, advised the NPC by letter that, "we are of course interested in learning what conclusions the Sub-committee reaches on the subject. But our general feeling is that it might be a mistaken policy to give the NATO Parliamentarians official status; and that if there were to be a move to create an Atlantic Assembly, it might be better to base it on O.E.C.D." The letter gave three reasons for this view: First, to create an assembly that must unavoidably be inhibited by security restrictions would cause frustration; secondly, the NPC was getting perhaps better results as an informal body than it would from an official status that might tend to put NATO "on the defensive"; and third, proliferation of assemblies was undesirable. Heath noted that this was not "a final and definitive expression of the opinion of H. M. G."[8]

This view is very close to that expressed by Dirk Stikker as Secretary General of NATO.[9] It was reconfirmed for the NPC investigators by R. W. J. Hooper, NATO's Assistant Secretary General for Political Affairs, who indicated the organization's satisfaction with the existing arrangements and warned that NATO officials would be compelled to give less information to an official assembly than they do to the NPC

---

[6]NPC, Special Subcommittee, Minutes, Copenhagen, June 29, 1963 (PC(63)24), p. 2.

[7]NPC, Working Group of Special Subcommittee, Minutes, Paris, May 27, 1963 (F.36, PC(63)12), Annex II, p. 1.

[8]Ibid., Annex I, p. 3.

[9]Cited above, Chapter 3, note 74.

because everything they said "would have to be cleared before-hand with the Member Nations."[10]

The French response was apparently transmitted orally. Boscher advised that the Foreign Minister agreed the NPC might "be given more powers and be better organised" but would object to the alteration of the NATO Treaty and to the idea of official status.[11] Earlier, the Chairman of the Working Group had reported:

> Mr. Couve de Murville had informed Mr. Boscher verbally that the French Government was in favour of an Atlantic Assembly based on the Council of Europe, plus America and Canada, an Assembly outside the scope of NATO activities, specifically concerned with OECD matters. The government did not oppose the idea of extending the powers of the NATO Parliamentarians' Conference, but would not accept a change in the Treaty requiring ratification. It rejected the idea of NATO plus the neutrals, for the same reason as the United Kingdom. [12]

The Dutch Foreign Minister advised that his government's position remained as it had been defined in 1962, viz.: "It may be remarked that the tendency of a number of the resolutions adopted by the NATO Citizens Convention forms a confirmation of the conceptions always advocated by the Government in NATO consultations. This is especially true as far as is concerned the desirability of strengthening and developing NATO as a political organization, the conversion of the Conference of NATO Parliamentarians into a consultative Atlantic Assembly . . . etc."[13]

The Norwegian member of the Subcommittee reported that according to the Foreign Minister, Norway "is most

---

[10]Ibid., Annex II, p. 2.

[11]NPC, Working Group of Special Subcommittee, Minutes, Copenhagen, June 29, 1963 (F.68 PC(63)21), p. 2.

[12]Ibid., May 27, 1963, p. 2.

[13]NPC, Report of the Subcommittee to be Submitted to the Standing Committee, undated (F.57 (Rev. 1) PC(63)20), Annex I, p. 1 (letter of May 22, 1963, from J. L. Kranenburg, Secretary of the Delegation, to Secretary of the NPC).

interested in the setting up of an Atlantic Assembly," but that the country

> felt herself in any case for the time being, obliged to work for a solution of the question according to those principles to which the country had given its support in the Council of Europe, i.e. a parliamentary assembly of the OECD which meets immediately before or after the NATO Parliamentarians' Conference, and which will have the same members from the U.S.A. and Canada, whilst it is intended that the European members be those who are also members of the Consultative Assembly of the Council of Europe.[14]

Luxembourg was reported as favoring official status for the NPC and as believing an Atlantic Assembly should be limited to the members of NATO.[15]

Apparently the only other country whose position emerged from the NPC inquiry was the United States. Lord Crathorne, then President of the Conference, told the Standing Committee in July 1963 that President Kennedy "had shown himself favourably inclined towards the creation of an Atlantic Assembly" and that Secretary of State Dean Rusk "had taken a very positive attitude." The Secretary had indicated that such an assembly should be competent to discuss all Atlantic questions, and that he would prefer the initiative for its establishment to come from the European countries.[16]

A document of unstated origin[17] (in fact, the Department of State) advised that the question was "essentially the interest and responsibility of the U.S. Congress," but that, "If the parliamentarians of other nations would find it desirable, we would be glad to see members of the U.S. Congress join in

---

[14]Ibid., Annex I, p. 2 (letter of May 24, 1963, from Sven Stray to the NPC Secretary).

[15]NPC, Standing Committee, Minutes, Copenhagen, July 1, 1963 (F.79 SC(63)22), p. 7.

[16]Ibid., p. 3.

[17]Ibid., "An Atlantic Parliamentary Assembly," Annex, June 25, 1963.

an examination of the possibilities of such an Assembly and would be willing to help in any way." The statement added that "The jurisdiction of such an Assembly should embrace all matters, world-wide, of interest to the Atlantic partnership, political, economic, cultural and military, including specifically NATO and the OECD." Membership should be limited to members of those two organizations and the new entity should be able to serve the interests of the NATO nations "at least as fully" as the NPC.

Congressman Wayne Hays, who has at times made himself a spokesman for both the Congress and the Executive on Atlantic parliamentary questions, corroborated that document. He told the Standing Committee in July 1963 that he "had no objection to the institutionalisation of the Conference. The United States was ready to go as far as the Europeans might suggest; but it felt there should be only one Atlantic organization with each country's representation being in relation to its population. . . . [An OECD parliament] would serve no useful purpose."[18] Hays had earlier advised the Subcommittee that the Americans "were opposed to a proliferation of international assemblies, and would even favour the merging of some of them."[19]

Congressman Hays has in fact generally appeared more skeptical of proposals to establish an Atlantic Assembly than have some of his colleagues and officials of the Department of State. It was Hays who proposed at the first meeting of the Subcommittee in March 1963 that steps be taken at the outset to ascertain the opinions of "appropriate officials of the governments concerned."[20] By June he had concluded, with a majority of the Working Group, that neither the "institutionalisation" of the NPC nor its conversion into an Atlantic Assembly appeared possible at that time.[21] While declaring that "he personally subscribed to the theory of a consultative

---

[18]NPC, Standing Committee, Minutes, Copenhagen, July 1, 1963, op. cit., p. 6.

[19]NPC, Special Subcommittee, Minutes, Paris, March 21, 1963 (F. 25, PC(63)8), p. 4.

[20]Ibid.

[21]NPC, Working Group, Minutes, Copenhagen, June 29, 1963, op. cit., p. 2.

assembly," he contributed significantly to the decision of the NPC against pursuing the proposal. He expressed the opinion that "it would not be possible at this time to pass the necessary legislation through Congress...." Representative John Lindsay disagreed with that appraisal of the outlook in Congress and suggested that the position of the U. S. delegation might have appeared quite different if the Senate group under Senator Fulbright had not been prevented by legislative responsibilities from attending the Ninth Session.[22]

DEFECTS OF THE NPC SUBCOMMITTEE'S INQUIRY

That exchange pointed up the essential defect of the inquiry undertaken by the Special Subcommittee. As Lord Silkin had suggested to the latter's Working Group in April, "It would be premature to consult governments until they [the Subcommittee] had something positive to put before them."[23] The fact is that the Subcommittee's Working Group dismissed the terms of reference given it by the Conference in 1962, undertook a task for which there had been no serious preparation, as well as no mandate, and put questions — or at any rate obtained answers — that were evidently based on divergent notions of what was to be proposed. The inquiry was conducted by different individuals in different capitals. It was carried out without any prior attempt to develop a clear and concrete proposal or to establish a consensus among interested parliamentarians.

The statements of most if not all of the governments cited leave room for the inference that an approach on a different basis might have yielded a rather different evaluation of the possibilities. In regard to the neutrals, for example, no systematic attempt appears to have been made to determine what degree of isolation from discussions of security affairs, or what variant of the two-tier formula, might in fact be acceptable. As will be suggested below, there is reason to

---

[22]NPC, Meeting of the Political Committee, Minutes, Paris, November 5, 1963 (Doc. F.190, PC(63)34), p. 5-7.

[23]NPC, Working Group, Minutes, Paris, April 26, 1963 (F.29 PC(63) 11), p. 6. Cf. Lord Crathorne to the same effect, ibid., March 21, 1963, p. 5.

believe that something less than complete dissociation might suffice. The real possibilities will remain obscure until wider consultations are undertaken on the basis of more fully defined alternatives.

ASSOCIATION OF THE NON-NATO MEMBERS
OF THE OECD

Of the OECD's twenty-one members, six — each for different reasons — are outside the Atlantic Alliance: Switzerland, Sweden, Austria, Ireland, Spain, and Japan. Only detailed consultations with the parliamentary and governmental leaders of those countries, on the basis of specific alternatives, would reveal to what extent or in what manner they may be prepared to take part in a consultative Atlantic Assembly. Advocates of such an assembly generally believe that a formula can be worked out. Some of them would add, however, that failure to agree on a means of associating the neutrals should not deter the others from proceeding with the establishment of the new assembly. They argue that the non-NATO countries of OECD (Japan apart) comprise less than ten percent of the OECD peoples; that the policies of the neutrals are evolving and may permit some of them sooner or later to accept a role in the proposed assembly; and that the countries sharing the NATO tie would be ill-advised to deprive themselves of the advantages of having a parliamentary body competent to advise in the economic and social as well as the military spheres.

Ireland, Japan, Spain

While Ireland has indicated no desire to join NATO, there is evidence that the Irish would not object to taking part in a consultative Atlantic Assembly having competence in security as well as other matters. Ireland has applied for accession to the Rome Treaty under Article 237 (full membership). In connection with that application, the Irish Prime Minister has stated publicly that his country accepted the political as well as the economic aims of the treaty:

> We are in full agreement with these political aims and we accept that they involve the commitment to participate in discussions and to cooperate in matters of defence. These commitments have not yet been defined,

but we have made no reservations with regard to
them. . . . We are not neutral and we wish to remove
any misunderstandings about Ireland's position in the
world.[24]

Japan's membership in the OECD gives the Japanese Diet
a valid claim to representation in interparliamentary activity
concerning OECD business. While Japan's membership, as
Livingston Hartley observes, enhances the importance of
OECD, it "adds to the difficulty of setting up an 'Atlantic'
Assembly."[25] One prominent observer has suggested that
the "difficulty" might be overcome by calling the new body
the Great Atlantic and Pacific Parliamentary Assembly! Some
who foresee and advocate the eventual federation of the Atlantic nations might be tempted to regard Japan's participation in an Atlantic Assembly as inconsistent with that line of
development. There can be no doubt, however, that the participation of Japanese legislators in the OECD discussions of
an Atlantic Assembly would in itself be appropriate and desirable. This need not in any practical sense impede the
Atlantic movement. The association of the Japanese should
be encouraged on the basis of the same two-tier formula that
has been suggested for other non-NATO members of the OECD.

Spain, like Japan, is a member of the OECD but not of
NATO. Spanish participation in an Atlantic Assembly would
not be precluded on grounds of either geography or neutrality.
Objections based on the character of the Spanish Government,
however, have been at least one reason for Spain's failure to
enter the Council of Europe and for the fact that her application in 1962 for association with the European Economic Community is expected to lead to something less than associate
status. The same sentiment among other governments and
parliaments could complicate Spain's admission to an Atlantic
Assembly. On the other hand, Portugal, which is a full member of NATO and the NATO Parliamentarians' Conference,
has been the object of similar reservations. Some alternative
to outright exclusion of one or both of these countries seems
worthy of consideration. As was suggested in the last chapter,

---

[24]Council of Europe, Consultative Assembly, Report on the General
Policy of the Council of Europe, by Pierre Pflimlin, Doc. 1545, January
15, 1963, p. 7-8.

[25]"Towards an Atlantic Assembly," The Atlantic Community Quarterly, Vol. 4, No. 1, Spring 1966, p. 110.

in connection with possible voting formulas for the proposed consultative Atlantic Assembly, one such alternative would be to offer a form of associate membership that might entail either a reduced number of delegates or the full number having the right to speak but not to vote.

The Problem of the European Neutrals

The problem of membership posed by assigning both defense and economic functions to a single Atlantic Assembly is thus confined to Sweden, Switzerland and Austria. Each of these countries has different views as to the compatibility of neutrality with participation in international organizations of various kinds, and in all three those views appear to be evolving. Thus Sweden and Austria are members of the United Nations, while Switzerland — a member of the League of Nations for 18 years — has remained outside. Switzerland has recently joined the Council of Europe, after nearly fourteen years of self-exclusion. What appears to be the common denominator of the neutral policies of these countries is, in the words of a recent Council of Europe study, an effort

> to create in time of peace the conditions they believe they require to be able, in the event of armed conflict breaking out, to remain neutral or, more precisely, to conform to the rules of the law of neutrality. In their political relations with other countries, the Neutrals consider that their status requires them to behave, even in time of peace, in such a way as to maintain confidence in their will and ability to remain neutral in the case of war.[26]

All three have applied for association rather than full membership in the European Economic Community in order to obtain certain derogations from the Rome Treaty. The requested derogations would permit the neutrals some freedom of action in trade policy toward third countries and authorize them to "suspend or denounce the association agreement if this appeared essential to protect their neutrality, in particular in the event of war or of a serious international crisis."[27]

---

[26]Council of Europe, Consultative Assembly, Memorandum on the Political Aspects of Neutrality by Paul Struye, Doc. 1581, April 29, 1963, p. 27-28. Hereinafter referred to as the Struye Memorandum.

[27]Ibid., p. 35. The applications are still pending.

There is no doubt that the governments and peoples of the European neutrals are wedded to their neutrality. Austria is committed to it by the State Treaty of 1955 which freed it from allied occupation. Switzerland's neutrality is likewise a matter of international law, under the settlement of the Congress of Vienna. Sweden's, like Switzerland's, has proved itself viable in two world wars. Sweden remains convinced, quite plausibly, that its neutrality is "a stabilizing and pacifying factor in Northern Europe." As the Struye memorandum observes, both Switzerland and Sweden believe that their respective positions as neutrals have enabled them to carry out in Europe and elsewhere "various tasks of arbitration and mediation" that could be assigned only to neutrals.

For those who desire to associate the European neutrals with the institutional development of the Atlantic community, the question need not be whether neutrality has become outmoded. The question is rather whether the conditions necessary for maintaining neutrality in peacetime have not in fact changed. Is it any longer realistic, asks Struye, for the neutrals "to make their policy comply with the need, even if unjustified, to maintain the necessary confidence of all potential belligerents? Is it realistic to count on the confidence of the Soviet bloc in a concept of neutrality which it does not share? Is it this confidence which dictates the present attitude of the U.S.S.R. towards European neutrals? Is it not rather dictated by the strength and solidarity of the free world?. . ." Thanks to the unification of Europe, Struye argues, "the age of European wars seems to be over. . . . European integration is therefore intended to abolish the state of affairs which necessitated a neutral policy as it was formerly conceived and as formerly it logically had to be conceived." Future wars would either be small wars outside of Europe, in which case they would be unlikely to affect the neutrals of Europe, or they will involve East and West in a major struggle, "which would in all probability be total and worldwide and which would expose all the participants to the risk of total destruction. . . ."[28] On this analysis, Sweden and Switzerland might well be able in fact to take part in additional European and Atlantic activities without compromising what is essential and valid with respect to their neutrality.

---

[28]Ibid., p. 31.

The debates on defense issues in the Consultative Assembly of the Council of Europe throw further light on what may be the limits of the neutrals' participation in European and Atlantic security.

Article 1(d) of the Statute of the Council of Europe states: "Matters relating to national defense do not fall within the scope of the Council of Europe." This provision has been interpreted in practice to mean that, while technical and military aspects of defense are proscribed, the Assembly is free to deal with the political aspects of European defense. The Assembly's guide in this regard was suggested by Harold Macmillan in 1950, namely that the Assembly can properly take up defense matters that would be handled in a national parliament by the minister of foreign affairs.[29] Thus, following the outbreak of the Korean War, the Assembly adopted a resolution proposed by Winston Churchill and Paul Reynaud for the creation of a European Army under a European Minister of Defense.[30] The Assembly has continued to deal with the "political aspects" of European defense, including the proposed European Defense Community and Western European Union.[31]

The question of the Assembly's competence in this field arose again in May 1963, in connection with a draft resolution of the Political Committee recommending that the Governments "envisage the organisation of a European nuclear defence within the framework of the Atlantic Alliance."[32] Upon protest of representatives of the neutrals, the proposal was modified to provide that there would be "set up in all political fields, including defence, a genuine partnership on a footing of equality between Europe and the United States of America."[33]

---

[29] Council of Europe, Consultative Assembly, 2d Session, Doc. 4, August 7, 1950, para. 45.

[30] Ibid., Texts Adopted, Recommendation 5, August 11, 1950.

[31] Ibid., Recommendation 53, November 24, 1950; Resolution 12, 1952; 21, 1952; 33, 1953; 63, 1954.

[32] Ibid., Doc. 1581.

[33] Ibid.

The fact that the parliamentarians and the governments of Sweden and Austria have not been deterred from full partici-pation in an organization that has dealt freely with the "po-litical aspects" of collective defense and that Switzerland has recently seen fit to join it suggests that agreement on a for-mula for associating the European neutrals with a consulta-tive Atlantic Assembly is not necessarily beyond the realm of the possible. Indeed, on the basis of conversations with a number of M.P.'s and officials from several OECD countries, Philander P. Claxton, a senior official of the Department of State, has concluded that "perhaps the warmest interest in an Atlantic Assembly was expressed by parliamentarians of the neutral nations." He found that these M.P.'s generally regard their countries as part of the Atlantic Community and feel "much less concern" than do the Foreign Office officials about the effect participation in an Atlantic Assembly might have on their countries' status as neutrals. It was also clear, however, that the neutrals' association with the assembly would have to be so arranged as to avoid participation and the appearance of participation in discussions of strictly military questions. [34]

The revolution of military technology, the bipolarization of international power, and the unification of Western Europe have modified the objective environment of European neutrality. The neutrals have begun adjusting their policies, and some forms of closer association with other Western countries are under official consideration. It would be premature to rule out the possibility of their association in an eventual consultative assembly serving the Atlantic Community as a whole.

THE PROBLEM OF U.S. PARTICIPATION

United States participation in the NATO Parliamentarians' Conference is authorized by a law dating from 1956 that, until 1963, limited both the number of delegates and the time they could devote to it. The Act stipulated that

---

[34] Claxton, op. cit., p. 9-10, 52-54, 64-72. For a Swiss view of the neutrals' dilemma, see Jacques Freymond, "The European Neutrals and the Atlantic Community," International Organization, Vol. XVII, No. 3, Summer 1963, p. 592-609.

not to exceed eighteen Members of Congress shall be appointed to meet jointly and annually, and when Congress is not in session, with representative parliamentary groups from other NATO members, for discussion of common problems in the interests of the maintenance of peace and security in the North Atlantic area. Of the Members of the Congress to be appointed for the purposes of this resolution (hereinafter designated as the "United States Group"), half shall be appointed by the Speaker of the House from Members of the House, and half shall be appointed by the President of the Senate from Members of the Senate. Not more than five of the appointees from the respective Houses shall be of the same political party.[35]

An amendment to that act in 1963 deleted the requirement that U. S. participants must take part only when Congress is not in session. The amendment was added in order to assure that the United States would be represented in the NPC session of November 4-8, 1963, notwithstanding the prospect that Congress would still be in session at that time.

The limit of 18 delegates remains. It would pose a serious problem in the event that the NPC were converted into a consultative Atlantic Assembly. As has been suggested above, the proposed metamorphosis of the NPC would almost certainly necessitate the adoption of a rule of "one delegate, one vote." If the number of U. S. delegates were made equal to the number of votes assigned to the U. S. in the NPC, the size of the American delegation would have to be doubled.

The establishment of a consultative Atlantic Assembly would necessitate an increase not only in the number of U. S. delegates but in the time they would be obliged to devote to its activities. The length of sessions depends upon several variables, including the adequacy of the staff, the effectiveness of committee work, the definition of the Assembly's competence and powers, and its success in confining its agendas and speakers to essentials. The Consultative Assembly of the Council of Europe meets four weeks a year, and it is likely that sessions of an Atlantic Assembly would run a minimum of two weeks and conceivably much longer. While some European M.P.'s have found it possible to devote

---

[35]P. L. 689, 84th Congress, July 11, 1956. The law authorizes an annual appropriation of $30,000 for expenses of the U. S. group.

as much as ninety days or more per year to international
parliamentary responsibilities, American legislators would
be hard put to allocate two weeks a year to such activity.
Although generally better equipped with staff than their European counterparts and free from the obligation to earn part
of their living in non-legislative pursuits, U. S. legislators
find themselves seriously restricted when it comes to participation in activities of this kind.[36]

Adequate U. S. participation in a full-fledged consultative
Atlantic Assembly would require some substantial adjust-
ments on the part of both the individual American delegate
and the Assembly.[37]   Efforts to limit agenda and speeches
would have to be more rigorous than has been the case in
the Council of Europe. Many of the committee sessions and
some of the plenaries would no doubt have to be held in or
near Washington. Committees would have to rely heavily on
the preparatory work of the Secretariat. It might even be
necessary, as was suggested in the Declaration of Paris and
discussed in Chapter 8, to permit the inclusion of some
non-parliamentarians in the national delegations. Other
measures, such as paired votes or proxy procedures might
also prove necessary. In the final analysis, there is little
doubt that establishment of a consultative Atlantic Assembly
would add to the burdens of already overburdened American
legislators. The latter will be bound to take that fact into full
account and to weigh it against the advantages that might
accrue to all concerned from the work of the proposed assembly.

RECOMMENDATIONS

The practical possibilities today for strengthening Atlantic
parliamentary consultation are limited because of the opposition expressed by certain governments to any reorganization
that would require adoption or amendment of treaties. More

---

[36]Cf. Carl Marcy, "The Role of Interparliamentary Bodies in the
Free World," (unpublished memorandum, 1962), p. 5-7.

[37]The same may be true with respect to Canadian participation.
See remarks by J. E. Dube, Canadian M.P., at meeting of NPC Political
Committee, Paris, November 5, 1963 (Doc. F.190 PC(63)34), p. 5.

recently, the very future of NATO has been put in doubt by
President De Gaulle's announcement of March 11, 1966, that
France would withdraw her forces from the integrated NATO
command and would evict the military headquarters from
French soil. In the circumstances, neither the establishment
of a consultative Atlantic Assembly, nor the conferring of official status on the NATO Parliamentarians' Conference,
appears immediately feasible.

This situation leaves reform-minded Atlantic parliamentarians with less ambitious alternatives. Three complementary lines of action now seem possible. One would be the
adoption of certain measures, as suggested in Chapters 3 and
5, to enhance the effectiveness of the present NATO Parliamentarians' Conference. Another, as noted in Chapter 7,
would be to adopt Pflimlin's proposal for an informal
arrangement permitting members of the NATO Parliamentarians' Conference and the Consultative Assembly of the
Council of Europe to meet periodically for joint discussions
of OECD and other appropriate matters. The third, which
looks to the longer run, and which might be facilitated by
the second, would be the preparation by a nucleus of Atlantic
parliamentarians and specialists of detailed plans for the
eventual rationalization of Western parliamentary consultation and the establishment of a consultative Atlantic Assembly.
All three lines of action could be initiated without substantial
delay.

A "Council of Wise Men"

Only occasionally, thus far, has the NPC been able to
make its recommendations so timely, concrete and constructive as to compel attention and action on the part of the governments and executive agencies concerned. A partial remedy
of this deficiency, it may be suggested, could be found in an
adaptation of a proposal that has been advanced in a variety
of forms in recent years, most notably by Lord Franks in
October 1962. What Lord Franks, taking a leaf from the experience of the European Economic Community, had suggested
was that

> If the Atlantic group of nations seriously wills the at-
> tainment of its broad political ends in the world and
> searches for common solutions to its economic prob-
> lems on the international scale, [it must adopt] political

procedures akin in some respects to those operating in the Six. . . . The partnership of the Atlantic group of nations cannot get where it wants simply by the established processes of cooperation and negotiation: conferences with the unanimity rule and the compromising out of agreement between national interests. The scale and the urgency of the problems no longer permit it. A new way has to be found: a new organization, institution or commission, which will have sufficient standing, independence and initiative to formulate common solutions and put them forward to the governments of the several nations of the group, so that they will have to face in argument not merely each other but also and at the same time the solution proposed for the partnership as a whole as best realizing its common good.[38]

The idea has something in common with Professor Kissinger's proposal for a "North Atlantic Council,"[39] with Sir Anthony Eden's call in 1961 for a "political general staff,"[40] with Professor Robert Bowie's "NATO steering committee,"[41] with Secretary Herter's "permanent High Council,"[42] and with Pierre Uri's "Council of Partnership" and group of "Wise Men."[43] All of these proposals contemplate the establishment

[38]Lord Franks, "Cooperation Is Not Enough," Foreign Affairs, Vol. 41, No. 1, October 1962, p. 33. Cited above, Chapter 8, note 9.

[39]Henry A. Kissinger, The Necessity for Choice: Prospects for American Foreign Policy (New York: Harper, 1960), p. 167.

[40]Speech to Young Conservatives, June 10, 1961, cited in J. W. Fulbright, "For a Concert of Free Nations," Foreign Affairs, Vol. 40, No. 1, October 1961, p. 11-12.

[41]Robert R. Bowie, "Tensions within the Alliance," Foreign Affairs, Vol. 42, No. 1, October 1963, p. 64.

[42]Op. cit., p. 306; also "Declaration of Paris," op. cit., Part I.

[43]Op. cit., p. 100-104. Cf. proposal by President de Gaulle for a "NATO Directorate," September 1958; also proposal by Jean Monnet's Action Committee for the United States of Europe for the establishment of a "Committee of Entente" between Europe and the United States "to prepare joint positions on problems as they call for action," as a step toward Atlantic partnership --- Joint Declaration, Bonn, June 1, 1964,

of a small, top-level official body with responsibility for varying mixes of planning, recommending and deciding on a regional scale. Uri's concept, inspired like that of Lord Franks by the EEC Commission, would establish a permanent group of three or four "outstanding public figures distinguished for their impartiality, imagination and experience, whose moral influence would make up for what they lacked in delegated authority." Their job would be to "give continuous attention to the most pressing problems of the moment" and to make recommendations that would be placed automatically on the agenda of the proposed bipartite ministerial Council of Partnership.

The proposals of Franks and Uri share with the others cited the perhaps transient defect of requiring intergovernmental approval to make them operative at a time when such approval appears remote. Yet there is little doubt that if a group such as that advocated by Franks or Uri were able to function even unofficially, it might assist materially in clarifying some key issues of Atlantic cooperation and in promoting a consensus for specific "next steps." Why not, then, ad interim, establish such a body as an unofficial adjunct to the NATO Parliamentarians' Conference?

The record of the NPC makes clear, as a number of its participants have complained, that its annual deliberations suffer severely from the lack of adequate information and of preparatory analysis of the most pertinent issues. Endowing the group with an independent Council of Wise Men disposing of the time, staff, and experience to prepare an annual review of Atlantic problems and to suggest proposals for debate would give the Conference a far more promising solution to its

---

p. 8-10; and ibid., May, 9, 1965. Cf. also recommendation by Representatives Henry S. Reuss (D., Wis.) and Robert F. Ellsworth (R., Kans.) that "The OECD should establish an executive commission independent of national governments and having the power to initiate proposals, make recommendations, and issue reports to the Organization as a whole." The Congressmen noted that "A high-level commission with the power and duty to make proposals for the Organization as a whole. as opposed to proposals from national governments, has worked well for the three European communities.... The recommendations of a distinguished commission of, perhaps, five 'wise men' would strengthen the ability of the Organization to make decisions in the common interest." --- Off Dead Center: Some Proposals to Strengthen Free World Economic Cooperation, a Report to the Joint Economic Committee, op. cit., p. 19.

dilemma than that of the Rapporteur-General approach adopted in the Ninth Session.

By the same token, a Council of Wise Men could hardly find a more promising forum and sounding board for its unofficial proposals than the NATO Parliamentarians' Conference. The combination might considerably enhance the effectiveness of Atlantic parliamentary activity.

There were some, including the present writer, who urged in 1960 that the Atlantic Institute assume such a "Wise Man" function unofficially for the Atlantic Community, and indeed that only by so doing could the Institute expect to perform a unique service readily distinguishable from the research and publication activities of such groups as the Council on Foreign Relations, the Royal Institute of International Affairs, the Centre d'Etudes de Politique Etrangère, the Instituto per gli Studie di Politici Internazionale, the Institute for Strategic Studies, the Overseas Development Institute, and others. The unique and significant function of an Atlantic Institute, it seemed then, would be "to give the Community a top-level, independent body of advisers able and willing to make policy choices and to defend them publicly (or, on occasion, in confidential reports)".[44]

Just as with the Monnet Committee, the effectiveness of the proposed unofficial Council of Wise Men for the Atlantic Community will depend upon the timeliness of the recommendations, the soundness of the policy choices, the prestige of the participants and the follow-up effort by the political leaders who take part in the process as members of the NATO Parliamentarians' Conference. It is likely that a Council of Wise Men thus conceived could count on substantial informal cooperation and information from those of the NATO Governments desirous of promoting Atlantic unity. The Atlantic Institute might have a role here in contributing some of the necessary research and staff services to such a group.

An Interparliamentary Study Group

Although parliamentarians and government officials have manifested a growing interest in the idea of a consultative

---

[44]Memorandum to William C. Foster, first Chairman of the U. S. Committee for the Atlantic Institute (now Atlantic Council of the United States), "Atlantic Institute: a Reappraisal," October 26. 1960, p. 4, by the present writer.

Atlantic Assembly and other measures for rationalizing interparliamentary organization, they have yet to undertake a
thorough exploration of the alternatives and the possibilities.
The decision of the NATO Parliamentarians in 1962 to make
such a study was not implemented. The Special Subcommittee
established for that purpose in effect altered its terms of
reference, and its report consequently offered no basis for
an adequate evaluation of the proposals or the prospects.[45]

A detailed report and plan should be drawn up by an ad hoc
study group of parliamentarians and specialists, setting forth
annotated recommendations on the establishment, structure,
composition, functions, powers and procedure of a consultative Atlantic Assembly, and of such interim arrangements as
may be deemed desirable.[46] The Study Group's report should
be based on systematic consultations with parliamentarians,
government officials and specialists in all Atlantic countries.
When published, the report of the Study Group would provide
a basis for wider discussion and for organized efforts to
promote the consensus needed to put its recommendations
into effect.

The Study Group would consist of European and American
parliamentarians and specialists in international organization.
A small staff would prepare a series of working papers
covering all aspects of the question for the consideration of
the Study Group. Much of this work could be undertaken by
correspondence, but a number of meetings of the Study Group
in Europe and the United States would have to be budgeted.

The work might be carried out in three phases. First,
the preparation by the Study Group of a draft of the report
and recommendations; distribution to selected specialists,
M.P.'s and officials in all countries concerned. Secondly, a
tour of the European and North American capitals by a Study
Group delegation, including the Chairman and Rapporteur,
for the purpose of consultations on the draft report with
appropriate members of parliament, specialists and foreign
office officials. Thirdly, publication of a final report incorporating the recommendations and commentary as revised in
the light of the consultations.

---

[45]See section above, "Defects of the NPC Subcommittee's Inquiry."

[46] The work should be done by a nucleus of Western parliamentarians
representing the European neutrals as well as the NATO allies. This
would preclude sponsorship by the NATO Parliamentarians' Conference.

Both technically and politically, an undertaking of this nature would lay the groundwork for official action against the time when that becomes feasible. As Spaak pointed out in 1959 when he made a similar recommendation, and as the present study has shown, the problems of interparliamentary reorganization are complex and difficult. Parliamentarians are both best qualified and best placed to present, in Spaak's words, "concrete proposals that the governments would be obliged to examine."[47]

CONCLUSIONS

Institutions are means to ends, not ends in themselves. It is beyond doubt that if the Atlantic Community were endowed with federal institutions, many of its present problems could be promptly overcome. But that presupposes agreement on some range of specific policy objectives, as well as a belief that a given institutional reform can bring those objectives closer to realization.

The task of statesmanship is neither to devise panaceas nor to negotiate agreement on platitudes but, as Harlan Cleveland, now U.S. Ambassador to NATO, has put it, to bring about such "next steps" as can be taken at a given moment to advance common purposes.[48] The "next step," in

[47]See Chapter 3 above. On August 12, 1965, Senator Jacob K. Javits endorsed the present proposal in a speech on the floor of the Senate, saying: "The United States Congress in cooperation with parliamentary leaders in Britain should take the lead in the formation of an ad hoc inter-parliamentary Working Group whose task would be: (a) to chart a course toward the establishment of a consultative Atlantic Assembly composed of both NATO countries and European neutrals; and (b) to develop a consensus among parliaments and governments in support of this idea...."--- "The New Battle of Britain," Congressional Record, August 12, 1965, p. 19423. Sir James Hutchinson of the United Kingdom, then President of the WEU Assembly, put forward a somewhat similar proposal in 1957. This was to establish a Joint Working Party, consisting of members of that assembly and officials of the national governments and parliaments to study ways and means of strengthening European parliamentary consultation. See WEU Doc. 62, op. cit., p. 13-14 and Doc. A/WEU/B(57)8.

[48]Speech before World Federation of UN Associations, "The Uses of Diversity," New York, N. Y., September 9, 1963.

a given conjuncture of circumstances, may be the settlement of a dispute or the adoption of a common project, or it may be the reform or establishment of an institution. When President Kennedy proposed a new partnership of equals between the United States and a United Europe, he said: "It will be achieved by concrete steps to solve the problems that face us all, military, economic and political. Partnership is not a posture but a process, a continuous process that grows stronger each year as we devote ourselves to common tasks."[49]

The need for more effective institutions among the Atlantic nations is widely recognized, and there has been no dearth of concrete proposals from leading statesmen and scholars. Some of the proposals are perhaps of a sufficiently technical nature to permit their early adoption. Others can be expected to materialize only in a more propitious political climate. In the present context of Atlantic relations, so staunch an advocate of a "true Atlantic Community" as Christian Herter has concluded that, as a minimum, there must be agreements on problems of nuclear strategy, plus some development of the proposed trade partnership, "before common political institutional mechanisms can usefully be discussed."[50]

It is apparent from even a cursory survey of the political factors that major obstacles will confront any early renewal of efforts to establish a consultative Atlantic Assembly or to rationalize in other ways the existing interparliamentary arrangements.

Some of the opposition or indifference, confirmed by individual parliamentarians, arises from the fear that such an assembly would have so little power or such restricted possibilities for significant action that the interest of key M.P.'s could not be sustained and that the resulting anticlimax might damage the cause of Atlantic unity. In other quarters the idea has found dissenters whose concern is that it might divert or undermine the movement for European integration and, in particular, the prospects of an eventual extension of

---

[49]Speech at Frankfort, June 25, 1963. He had put forward the partnership concept a year earlier, in his speech at Philadelphia, July 4, 1962.

[50]Christian A. Herter, "Atlantica," op. cit., p. 304-305.

the European Economic Community to include Britain and other members of the European Free Trade Association.[51]

There is some opposition or indifference among certain U. S. legislators. While perhaps most Congressional leaders would support a comprehensive consultative Atlantic Assembly, some are impressed with the difficulties to be anticipated in attempting to associate the European neutrals or in assuring an adequate participation of American legislators and would prefer on such grounds among others to retain the informality and comparative simplicity of the present organization of NATO parliamentarians.

The most significant opposition, however, comes from the French Government, whose purpose is to reduce rather than to augment "Anglo-Saxon" influence in Europe. As the NATO Parliamentarians' Conference concluded in November 1963, it was President de Gaulle's veto of British membership in the EEC and the "prevailing uncertainty" among NATO allies as to each other's intentions that made the NPC's own project impractical for the present.[52]   De Gaulle's subsequent repudiation of important features of the Atlantic Alliance has, as noted above, dimmed still further the immediate prospects.

While, therefore, a substantially more rational ordering of the West's interparliamentary activity will have to await the development of a broader consensus regarding "Atlantic" policy objectives, there are, as this study has sought to show, distinct possibilities for devising more effective organization, and these might usefully be explored meanwhile by parliamentarians. To date, only sporadic quasi-official efforts have been made to study the alternatives and to ascertain the attitudes of the parliaments and the foreign ministries. A full airing of the issues and the possibilities with respect to rationalization would make it possible at least to chart an optimum course and perhaps to develop additional pressure for embarking upon it.

---

[51]See esp. WEU Assembly, 3d Session, The Unification of European Assemblies, Doc. 62, Report of General Affairs Committee (J. M. van der Goes van Naters, Rapporteur), September 21, 1957, p. 4 and 10-11.

[52]See Chapter 1 above. Cf. Claxton, op. cit., p. 53-56; and H. Field Haviland, "Building a Political Community," International Organization, Vol XVII, No. 3, Summer 1963, p. 750-751.

It has been argued in the present study that the NATO
Parliamentarians and the Atlantic Convention of NATO nations were right in proposing that the West needs essentially
no more than two international assemblies, one for the European Community and the other for the Atlantic "partnership."
It was further suggested that notwithstanding the continued
uncertainty as to Britain's eventual role in Europe, there is
no longer much of a case for a non-supranational "Greater
Europe" as a concept of regional organization and that accordingly the Consultative Assembly of the Council of Europe,
together with the Assembly of Western European Union and
the NATO Parliamentarians' Conference, might well be con-
solidated into a consultative Atlantic Assembly having a formal
relationship with both the North Atlantic Council and the OECD.
That this would pose serious difficulties and incur strenuous
opposition is amply clear, but there is reason to believe that
such a development could reinforce Atlantic cooperation and
do so without injury, and indeed with benefit, to European
integration.

It is this very prospect that makes such reform "unrealistic" in the present political context. The lack of consensus on Atlantic policy among the NATO governments is a
far more formidable obstacle than the uncertainties of the
European neutrals, whose possibilities of association with an
Atlantic Assembly under some variant of the two-tier formula
may be greater than they seem — and have yet, in any case,
to be adequately explored by those concerned.

The present political circumstances would appear to leave
Atlantic parliamentarians with the possibility of, as this study
has suggested, three complementary lines of interim effort.
One, as proposed by Pflimlin, would be to institute more or
less informal joint meetings of North American delegates to
the NPC with representatives of the Consultative Assembly
of the Council of Europe for the purpose of discussing Atlantic
economic problems and the business of the Organization for
Economic Cooperation and Development.

The second interim measure, which might best be carried
out under the sponsorship of such joint sessions, would be to
establish an interparliamentary study group to prepare detailed plans for a thorough rationalization of Western parliamentary consultation and to provide a basis for developing
the degree of governmental and parliamentary consensus
necessary to assure eventual implementation.

The third interim measure would be to strengthen the influence of the NATO Parliamentarians' Conference within the limitations of its present quasi-official status. Although the NPC is now studying the possibility of acquiring official status, the current uncertainties as to the future of NATO itself suggest that this project will encounter many of the same political obstacles that blocked Congressman Lindsay's proposal for an official Atlantic Assembly based on the wider membership of the OECD. If this estimate proves correct, the NPC will have to fall back temporarily on less drastic reforms, but these could prove of considerable importance.

An easing of the NPC's severe budgetary restrictions would pave the way for what might prove to be the two most significant steps the NATO parliamentarians could take to make their work more effective pending a change in the political climate and an opportunity for more fundamental reorganization. One would be to adapt to its own purposes the national follow-up procedures, discussed above in Chapter 5, that have been successfully pioneered by the Consultative Assembly in Strasbourg. The other would be to endow the Conference in effect with an independent "Council of Wise Men" of the sort that in one form or another has figured in so many recent proposals for the reform of NATO, notably that of Lord Franks in 1962. For this purpose a small, high-level, unofficial, well-staffed international committee, perhaps assisted by the Atlantic Institute, would be in effect attached to the Conference with the task of drawing up an annual review of Atlantic problems and of formulating proposals for consideration and debate in the Conference. This could, it is suggested, provide a more adequate solution than that adopted by the NATO Parliamentarians in 1963, namely the designation of a Rapporteur General, and would give fresh impetus and wider impact to Atlantic parliamentary consultation.

Atlantic parliamentary consultation, while far less developed than the European variety, has recorded some important achievements, and it seems clear that the question of making it a more significant factor in Atlantic cooperation will remain "on the agenda." The steps proposed here should lead eventually to others. The relationship between Europe and North America is based on a common heritage and shared values. It is evolving. New issues have emerged and others have been reformulated in the fields of trade, payments, foreign aid, political consultation, military strategy, management of the atomic deterrent and the structure of the Atlantic Community. These issues will compel the Western nations, despite current differences, to probe together more broadly and more deeply than ever before the opportunities and limitations of common action. A more effective association of European and North American parliamentarians would materially advance that process.

Reasonable men may differ as to the form in which future Atlantic cooperation should be organized. But they can perhaps agree that the hope of the whole free world, developed and developing nations alike, lies in the ever closer association and economic growth of Western Europe and North America. The remarkable if still incomplete success of the movement toward European unity — in which the European interparliamentary assemblies have played a significant part — has made more urgent as well as more promising the current efforts to develop an Atlantic "partnership." The further integration of the European Community, and its extension to other countries of Western Europe now desiring to participate, will enable the Europeans to join more effectively with the North Americans in meeting the world-wide responsibilities that they have jointly or severally assumed. Today's "disarray" among the Atlantic nations results from imperfect perceptions of national interest, which in an age of interdependence, must embrace the interests of others. Properly conceived and sponsored, Atlantic parliamentary consultation can promote better public understanding of the issues and the alternatives and give legislators on both sides of the Atlantic new opportunities, as President Johnson put it with reference to American foreign policy, "to share the lead in the search for new and stronger patterns of cooperation."[53]

---

[53]Statement at the White House, New York Times, April 5, 1964.

BIBLIOGRAPHY

Documents

Conte, Arthur. Draft Additional Protocol to the North Atlantic Treaty. Submitted to NATO Parliamentarians' Conference, 1961.

Council of Europe. Arrangement between the Council of Europe and the Organisation for Economic Co-operation and Development. Strasbourg: November 1962.

_____. Balance Sheet of the Work of the Council of Europe. Strasbourg: Directorate of Information, 1956.

_____. Chart Showing the Deposit of Ratifications of Council of Europe Conventions and Agreements. November 1964.

_____. Conference of Strasbourg Between Delegations of the Congress of the United States of America and of the Consultative Assembly of the Council of Europe. Official Record of Debates. Strasbourg: November 19-23, 1951.

_____. The Consultative Assembly: Procedure and Practice. 4th ed. Strasbourg: 1961.

_____. The European Convention on Human Rights. Strasbourg: 1952.

_____. European Co-operation: A New Definition of the Role of the Council of Europe, Statement by the Secretary-General (Strasbourg: May 1965).

_____. Man in a European Society: Programme of Work for the Intergovernmental Activities of the Council of Europe, adopted by the Committee of Ministers on May 2nd, 1966 (Strasbourg: Directorate of Information, 1966).

_____. Procedure of the Consultative Assembly. Strasbourg: 1953.

_____. Ten Years of the Council of Europe. Strasbourg: 1960.

_____. Texts of a Statutory Character Adopted by the Committee of Ministers in the Course of its Eighth and Ninth Sessions Revised with a View to their Ultimate Inclusion in a Revised Statute. Strasbourg, May and August 1951. London: H. M. Stationary Office, Command 118.

187

Council of Europe, Committee of Ministers. (Selected reports and resolutions.)

Council of Europe, Consultative Assembly. Aide-Memoire Concerning the Organisation of Parliamentary Debates Among Representatives of the Member Countries of OECD. (By Pierre Pflimlin). Document 1721, February 10, 1964.

_____ . Annual Reports on the Activities of the Permanent Working Party on Parliamentary and Public Relations (1957-65).

_____ . Documents of the Assembly. (1949-65).

_____ . Memorandum on the Political Aspects of Neutrality. (Paul Struye, Rapporteur). Document 1581, April 29, 1963.

_____ . Official Report of Debates. (1949-65).

_____ . Report on the Institutional Reform of the Council of Europe. (H. Teitgen, Rapporteur). Document 763, December 20, 1957.

_____ . Report on the Organisation of Parliamentary Debates on OECD Affairs. (Rapporteurs: Pierre Pflimlin and Alois Zimmer). Document 1546. January 15, 1963.

_____ . Report on Relations Between the Consultative Assembly and National Parliaments. Document 529 (Dehousse Memorandum), September 8, 1956.

European Economic Community. Parlement Européen, Reglement.

_____ . Annuaire-Manuel du Parlement Européen.

_____ . Débats.

_____ . Journal Officiel.

_____ . Rapport sur les compétences et les pouvoirs du Parlement Européen. Document 31, June 14, 1963.

Kennedy, President John F. Speech at Frankfort, Germany, June 25, 1963.

_____ . Speech at Philadelphia, July 4, 1962.

London and Paris Agreements, September-October 1954. Washington: Department of State, November 1954.

NATO Parliamentarians' Conference. Meetings of Committees. (1955-65). (Verbatim or summary reports.)

NATO Parliamentarians' Conference. Plenary Sessions. (1955–65).
    (Verbatim Reports).

_____ . Reports and Recommendations.

_____ . Rules of Procedure.

Non-Military Co-operation in NATO. Text of Report of the Com-
    mittee of Three. Paris: NATO Information Service, De-
    cember 13, 1956.

Protocol on Relations with the Council of Europe, Treaty Estab-
    lishing European Coal and Steel Community. In European
    Yearbook, Vol. I. The Hague: Martinus Nijhoff, 1955.

Treaty Establishing the European Atomic Energy Community
    (EURATOM) and Connected Documents. March 25, 1957.
    (Secretariat of the Interim Committee for the Common
    Market and EURATOM, Brussels).

Treaty Establishing the European Economic Community and Con-
    nected Documents. March 25, 1957. (Secretariat of the
    Interim Committee for the Common Market and EURATOM,
    Brussels).

Treaty of Economic, Social and Cultural Collaboration and Col-
    lective Self-Defense. Brussels: March 17, 1948.

U.S. Congress. Atlantic Union Resolutions. Hearings before the
    International Organization Affairs Subcommittee of the
    Committee on Foreign Relations, U. S. Senate, 89th Con-
    gress, 2nd Session, March 23 and 24, 1966.

_____ . Congressional Record. May 17, 1963; April 23, 1963.

_____ . Greater Cooperation Among Atlantic Democracies.
    Hearing before the Committee on Foreign Relations, U. S.
    Senate, 86th Congress, 2d Session, on Senate Concurrent
    Resolution 17 (re Atlantic Convention of NATO Nations)
    January 19, 1960.

_____ . Off Dead Center: Some Proposals to Strengthen Free
    World Economic Cooperation, 89th Congress, 1st Session,
    December, 1965 (Report of Joint Economic Committee).

_____ . P. L. 689. 84th Congress, July 11, 1956. As amended
    1963.

U. S. Congress, House of Representatives. House Concurrent Reso-
    lution 425 (87th Congress, 2d Session), February 19,
    1962.

_____ . House Concurrent Resolution 87 (88th Congress, 1st
    Session), February 7, 1963.

U.S. Congress, House of Representatives. Report of the United States House Delegation to the [First through Tenth] Conference of Members of Parliament from the NATO Countries.

U.S. Congress, Senate. Conduct of National Security Policy, Reports and Hearings by the Subcommittee on National Security and International Operations of the Government Operations Committee, 89th Congress, 1965–66.

_____ . Problems and Trends in Atlantic Partnership. Staff Study, Committee on Foreign Relations — I (September) 14, 1962. Document 132) and II (June 17, 1963, Document 21).

_____ . Report of the United States Senate Delegation to the [First through Eleventh] Conference of Members of Parliament from the NATO Countries.

U.S. Congress, U.S. Citizens Commission on NATO. Report to Congress. House Document 433, June 18, 1962.

Western European Union, Assembly. Aide-Memoire relatif a l'Assemblée de Défense Occidentale. (By Noel Salter). Document A/P 796, July 14, 1958.

_____ . Charter and Rules of Procedure of the Assembly of Western European Union, 1957.

_____ . Document Covering the Study by the Council of WEU of the Rationalisation of European Assemblies. Third Report of Council to Assembly. Document 79, Appendix I, February 21, 1958.

_____ . European Assemblies: The "Grand Design" (General Affairs Committee). Document 45, April 5, 1957.

_____ . The Future Organisation of Western Defence on the Executive and Parliamentary Levels. (Committee on Defence Questions and Armaments). Document 231, May 3, 1962.

_____ . Future Pattern of Europe. (General Affairs Committee), June 1962.

_____ . Practice and Procedure, July 1958.

_____ . Proceedings: Assembly Documents. (1955–65).

_____ . Proceedings: Minutes, 1956–65.

Western European Union, Assembly. Rationalisation of European Institutions Other Than Those of the Six. (Wigny Memorandum). Document A/WEU/CP (59) 6, May 15, 1959.

_____ . Rationalisation of European Parliamentary Institutions. (General Affairs Committee). Document 91, June 13, 1958.

_____ . State of European Security, 1956–61. (Committee on Defence Questions and Armaments). Document 215, November 10, 1961.

_____ . The Unification of European Assemblies. (J. M. van der Goes van Naters, Rapporteur, General Affairs Committee). Document 62, September 21, 1957.

Books

Acheson, Dean. Power and Diplomacy. Cambridge, Mass.: Harvard University Press, 1958.

_____ . Morning and Noon. Boston, Mass.: Houghton Mifflin, 1965.

Ball, Margaret M. NATO and the European Union Movement. London: Stevens & Sons (for the London Institute of World Affairs), 1959.

Beloff, Max. The United States and the Unity of Europe. Washington, D. C.: Brookings Institution, 1963.

Benoit, Emile. Europe at Sixes and Sevens: The Common Market, The Free Trade Association, and the United States. New York: Columbia University Press, 1961.

Beugel, E. H. van der. From Marshall Aid to Atlantic Partnership. New York: Elsevier Publishing Co., 1966.

Birke, Wolfgang. European Elections by Direct Suffrage: A Comparative Study of the Electoral Systems Used in Western Europe and Their Utility for the Direct Election of a European Parliament. Leyden: Sythoff, 1961.

Birrenbach, Kurt. The Future of the Atlantic Community. New York: Frederick A. Praeger, 1963.

Buchan, Alastair. NATO in the 1960's. London: Weidenfeld and Nicolson (for the Institute for Strategic Studies), 1960.

Camps, Miriam. Britain and the European Community. Princeton, N. J.: Princeton University Press, 1964.

Cerny, Karl H. and Briefs, Henry W. (eds.). NATO in Quest of Cohesion. New York: Frederick A. Praeger, 1965.

Cottrell, Alvin J., and Dougherty, James E. The Politics of the Atlantic Alliance. New York: Frederick A. Praeger, 1964.

Deutsch, Karl W., et al. Political Community and the North Atlantic Area. Princeton, N. J.: Princeton University Press, 1957.

European Movement and the Council of Europe. Forewords by Winston S. Churchill and Paul-Henri Spaak. London: Hutchinson & Co., 1949.

European Organisations. London: Political and Economic Planning, 1959.

European Yearbook. The Hague: Martinus Nijhoff. Annual volumes from 1955.

Fulbright, J. William. Prospects for the West. Cambridge, Mass.: Harvard University Press, 1963.

Furniss, Edgar S., Jr. (ed.). The Western Alliance: Its Status and Prospects. Ohio State University Press, 1965.

Graubard, Stephen R. (ed.). A New Europe. Boston, Mass.: Houghton Mifflin, 1964. Esp. "The Evolution of European Parliaments," by Alfred Grosser, and "Problems of Parliamentary Democracy in Europe," by Karl Dietrich Bracher.

Haas, Ernest B. Consensus Formation in the Council of Europe. Berkeley and Los Angeles: University of California Press, 1960.

Haviland, H. Field, Jr. (ed.). The U. S. and the Western Community. Haverford, Pa.: Haverford College Press, 1957.

Herter, Christian A. Toward an Atlantic Community. New York: Harper & Row (for the Council on Foreign Relations), 1963.

Ismay, Lord. NATO: The First Five Years, 1949–1954. Netherlands: Bosch-Utrecht, 1954.

Kissinger, Henry A. The Necessity for Choice: Prospects of American Foreign Policy. New York: Harper & Row, 1960.

————. The Troubled Partnership: A Reappraisal of the Atlantic Alliance. New York: McGraw-Hill, 1965.

Kleiman, Robert. Atlantic Crisis: American Diplomacy Confronts a Resurgent Europe. New York: W. W. Norton & Co., 1964.

Knorr, Klaus, (ed.). NATO and American Security. Princeton, N. J.: Princeton University Press, 1959.

Kraft, Joseph. The Grand Design. New York: Harper & Row, 1962.

Lawson, Ruth C., (ed.). International Regional Organisations: Con-
    stitutional Foundations. New York: Frederick A. Praeger,
    1962.

Lindsay, Kenneth. European Assemblies: The Experimental Period,
    1949-1959. London: Stevens & Sons, 1960.

————. Towards a European Parliament. Strasbourg: Council
    of Europe, 1958.

Mayne, Richard. The Community of Europe. London: Victor
    Gollancz, 1962.

Middleton, Drew. The Supreme Choice: Britain and Europe. New
    York: Alfred A. Knopf, 1963.

Moore, Ben T. NATO and the Future of Europe. New York: Harper
    & Row (for the Council on Foreign Relations), 1958.

NATO: Facts about the North Atlantic Treaty Organization. Paris:
    NATO Information Service, January 1962.

The Organisation for Economic Co-operation and Development.
    Paris: OECD Publications, 1963.

Philip, André. L'Europe unie et sa place dans l'économie inter-
    nationale. Paris: Presses universitaires de France, 1953.

Price, Roy. The Political Future of the European Community. Lon-
    don: John Marshbank, 1962.

Rencki, Georges. L'Assemblée Consultative du Conseil de l'Europe.
    Paris: Union Federaliste Interuniversitaire, 1956.

Robertson, A. H. The Council of Europe: Its Structure, Functions
    and Achievements. New York: Frederick A. Praeger, 1956.

————. European Institutions. London: Stevens & Sons, 1959.

————. Human Rights in Europe. Dobbs Ferry, N.Y.: Oceana
    Publications, 1963.

Sperling, Dietrich. Der Parlamentarische Charakter Europaischer
    Versammlungen. Leyden: A. W. Sythoff, 1961.

Stanley, Timothy W. NATO in Transition: The Future of the Atlantic
    Alliance. New York: Frederick A. Praeger, 1965.

Strang, Lord. Home and Abroad. London: Andre Deutsch, 1956.

Strausz-Hupé, Robert, Dougherty, James E., and Kintner, William R. Building the Atlantic World. New York: Harper and Row, 1963.

Uri, Pierre. Partnership for Progress: A Program for Transatlantic Action. New York: Harper & Row (for the Atlantic Institute), 1963.

Weil, Gordon L. The European Convention on Human Rights. Leyden: A. W. Sythoff, 1963.

Wendt, Frantz. The Nordic Council and Co-operation in Scandinavia. Copenhagen: Munksgaard, 1959.

White, Theodore H. Fire in the Ashes: Europe in Mid-Century. New York: William Sloane Associates, 1953.

Wilcox, Francis O., and Haviland, H. Field (eds.). The Atlantic Community: Progress and Prospects. New York: Frederick A. Praeger, 1963.

Wolfers, Arnold (ed.). Alliance Policy and the Cold War. Baltimore, Md.: Johns Hopkins Press, 1959.

Articles and Pamphlets

Acheson, Dean. "The Practice of Partnership," Foreign Affairs, Vol. 41, No. 2, January 1963, p. 247-260.

Atlantic Community Development Group for Latin America (ADELA). Memorandum, September 16, 1963. 6 pp.

————. Report of Executive Directors, April 1964. 32 pp.

————. General Information (brochure, n.d.)

Atlantic Congress Report. London: 1959. 95 pp.

Atlantic Convention of NATO Nations. Declaration of Paris. January 19, 1962. 17 pp.

Bowie, Robert R. "Tensions Within the Alliance," Foreign Affairs, Vol. 42, No. 1, October 1963, p. 49-69.

Conference on North Atlantic Community. Bruges, September 8-14, 1957. 23 pp.

Direct Elections of the European Parliament. London: Political and Economic Planning, October 24, 1960.

Les élections européennes au sufrage universel. Colloque des 16 et 15 avril 1960. Editions de l'Institut de Sociologie Solvay, 1960. 316 pp.

European Community, Information Service. The Facts. September 1962. 24 pp.

————. European Community. Washington: July–August 1963.

Franks, Lord. "Cooperation is Not Enough," Foreign Affairs, Vol. 41, No. 1, October 1962, p. 24–35.

Freymond, Jacques. "The European Neutrals and the Atlantic Community," International Organization, Vol. XVII, No. 3, Summer 1963, p. 529–609.

Fulbright, J. W. "For a Concert of Free Nations," Foreign Affairs, Vol. 40, No. 1, October 1961, p. 1–18.

Harned, Joseph. "Atlantic Assembly — A Genesis," Atlantic Community Quarterly, Vol. 3, No. 1, Spring, 1965, p. 43–49.

———— and Mally, Gerhard. Atlantic Assembly: Proposals and Prospects. London: Hansard Society, 1965. 29 pp. and appendices.

Hartley, Livingston. "A North Atlantic Assembly: Its Purpose, Function and Structure," Freedom and Union, Washington: January 1953, p. 1–11.

————. "Possible Step to Atlantic Unity," Freedom and Union, Washington: November 1951. 3 pp.

Haviland, H. Field. "Building a Political Community," International Organization, Vol. XVII, No. 3, Summer 1963, p. 733–752.

Herter, Christian A. "Atlantica," Foreign Affairs, Vol. 41, No. 2, January 1963, p. 299–309.

Hovey, J. Allan, Jr. "Obstructionism and the Rules of the General Assembly," International Organization, Vol. V, No. 3, August 1951, p. 515–530.

————. "Voting Procedure in the General Assembly," International Organization, Vol. IV, No. 3, August 1950, p. 412–427.

————. Report from Strasbourg. American Committee on United Europe. January 1953. 31 pp.

————. "Britain and the Unification of Europe," International Organization, Vol. IX, No. 3, August 1955, p. 1–15.

Hyman, Sidney. "In Search of 'The Atlantic Community'." New York Times Magazine, May 6, 1962, p. 17, 111, 114.

Kissinger, Henry. "Strains on the Alliance," Foreign Affairs, Vol. 41, No. 2, January 1963, p. 261-285.

McLachlan, Donald and de Freitas, Geoffrey. NATO Is Not Enough: Two Approaches to an Atlantic Assembly. London: Friends of Atlantic Union, 1955.

Mower, A. Glenn. "The Official Pressure Group of the Council of Europe." International Organization, Vol. XVIII, No. 2, Spring 1964, p. 292-306.

The North Atlantic Treaty Organization Parliamentarians' Conference, 1955-59. Foreword by Geoffrey de Freitas, M.P. London: The Hansard Society for Parliamentary Government, 1960. 47 pp.

NATO and the Peoples. Report of the First International Study Conference on the Atlantic Community, Oxford, September 7-13, 1952. London: British Society for International Understanding.

————. Report of the Second International Study Conference on the Atlantic Community, Copenhagen, August 30-September 5, 1953. London: British Society for International Understanding.

Oudenhove, Guy van. The Political Parties in the European Parliament: The First Ten Years (September 1952-September 1962). Leyden: Sijthoff, 1965.

The Parliament of the European Communities. London: Political and Economic Planning, March 9, 1964. 119 pp.

Poher, Alain. "Le Parlement Européen au Service de la Communauté," Courrier Européen, Avril-Mai-Juin, 1966, p. 1-2.

Roper, Elmo and Associates. American Attitudes Toward Ties With Other Democratic Countries. Washington: Atlantic Council of the United States, June 1964. 115 pp.

Schwelb, Egon. "On the Operation of the European Convention on Human Rights," International Organization, Vol. XVIII, No. 3, Summer 1964, p. 558-585.

Shuckburgh, Sir Evelyn. "Political Consultation." Paris: NATO Information Service, May 1960.

Weil, Gordon L. "The Evolution of the European Convention on Human Rights," American Journal of International Law, Vol. 57, No. 4, October 1963. 25 pp.

Unpublished Material

Claxton, Philander P., Jr., Prospects for an Atlantic Parliamentary Assembly. (Study for the Fifth Senior Seminar in Foreign Policy, Foreign Service Institute, Department of State), Washington: June 1963. 116 pp.; appendix, 74 pp.

Council on Foreign Relations, New York. Discussion Group, 1963. Confidential minutes and memoranda on proposals for an Atlantic Assembly.

Hartley, Livingston. "Development of the NATO Parliamentarians' Conference into an Atlantic Assembly." March 14, 1962.

Hovey, J. Allan, Jr. "Atlantic Institute: A Reappraisal," (memorandum) October 26, 1960. 8 pp.

Le Breton, J.-M. Le Contrôle Parlementaire de la Défense dans l'Alliance Atlantique (Ms. June 1963).

Marcy, Carl. "The Role of Interparliamentary Bodies in the Free World," (memorandum) 1962. 8 pp.

Moore, Walden (Director of Declaration of Atlantic Unity), letter to Lord Crathorne, May 6, 1963. 4 pp.

United Kingdom. Scheme for a General Parliamentary Assembly for Europe. (Foreign Office Memorandum.) April 5, 1957. 3 pp.

ABOUT THE AUTHOR

J. Allan Hovey, Jr. is Washington director of Allen and Murden, Inc., a firm of international public affairs and government relations consultants based in New York. Before joining the company early in 1965, he spent five years in Washington as government relations representative of Olin International.

He has served as a study director with the Council on Foreign Relations, as an administrative assistant in the executive office of the United Nations Secretary General, and as executive director of the American Committee on United Europe.

Dr. Hovey was graduated with high honors and Phi Beta Kappa from Swarthmore College in 1948. He received his M.A. and Ph.D. in international relations and law at Columbia University. He has also studied at McGill University and the Institut Universitaire de Hautes Etudes Internationales in Geneva, Switzerland.

He is a member of the Council on Foreign Relations, and is a founding member of the Board of Directors of the Atlantic Council of the United States. He served on the U.S. advisory group to the chairman of the Economic Committee of the NATO Parliamentarians' Conference. He has lived and traveled in Europe, Africa and the Far East and is the author of numerous articles in the field of international affairs.